Nature's Temples

Nature's Temples

A Natural History
of Old-Growth Forests

Revised and Expanded

Joan Maloof

Illustrated by Andrew Joslin

PRINCETON UNIVERSITY PRESS

Princeton and Oxford

Other books by Joan Maloof

Teaching the Trees: Lessons from the Forest
Among the Ancients: Adventures in the Eastern Old-Growth Forests
The Living Forest: A Visual Journey into the Heart of the Woods
Treepedia: A Brief Compendium of Arboreal Lore

Published by Princeton University Press
41 William Street, Princeton, New Jersey 08540
99 Banbury Road, Oxford OX2 6JX

press.princeton.edu

Library of Congress Cataloging-in-Publication Data
Names: Maloof, Joan, 1956– author. | Joslin, Andrew, illustrator.
Title: Nature's temples : a natural history of old-growth forests / Joan Maloof ; illustrated by Andrew Joslin.
Description: Expanded and revised edition. | Princeton, NJ : Princeton University Press, [2023] | Includes bibliographical references and index.
Identifiers: LCCN 2022026589 (print) | LCCN 2022026590 (ebook) | ISBN 9780691230504 (pbk.) | ISBN 9780691230702 (e-book)
Subjects: LCSH: Old growth forests. | Biodiversity. | BISAC: NATURE / Plants / Trees | NATURE / Ecology
Classification: LCC SD387.O43 M33 2016 (print) | LCC SD387.O43 (ebook) | DDC 333.75—dc23/eng/20220923
LC record available at https://lccn.loc.gov/2022026589
LC ebook record available at https://lccn.loc.gov/2022026590

British Library Cataloging-in-Publication Data is available

Cover illustrations and frontispiece by Andrew Joslin

This book has been composed in Lyon Text

Printed on recycled paper

Printed in the United States of America

10 9 8 7 6 5 4 3 2 1

In memory of William Landy Cook III (Will)

November 17, 1942—November 27, 2021

Contents

Preface

Forests have sprung naturally from the earth with no help required from humans. Although trees are the most obvious part of a forest, many, many other life forms exist there as well. The measure of this variety of life forms is termed biodiversity. The past ten thousand years have seen a drastic reduction in biodiversity due to human activities, primarily the way we manipulate the land. Many species have disappeared completely. Harvesting wood products from forests is one way that humans affect the land. In this book we look specifically at how the life forms in an ancient undisturbed forest, including the trees, differ from the life forms in a forest manipulated by humans. The details are shared in these pages, but I will give you the conclusion up front: more species exist in old-growth forests than in the forests we manage for wood products, and some species exist only in older forests.

In the chapters ahead you will frequently see old-growth forests compared to managed forests, so perhaps it is useful to clarify these terms right away. The forests that have formed naturally over a long period of time with little or no disturbance we call old-growth forests. In contrast, managed forests are the result of purposeful human action. Management techniques include logging, thinning, burning, planting, and spraying. Forests can be managed in many different ways and for many different reasons, but most often they are managed to grow timber for particular wood products that result in a financial return.

Although wood is a wonderful renewable resource, and most owners of forestland are now careful to replant after harvesting, it is a misconception that typical forest management can conserve all forest biodiversity. Scientific evidence tells us otherwise. In these pages I present the evidence. The studies that enable us to challenge the misconception are sprinkled far and wide among many different journals and over many years, so I thought it helpful to compile descriptions of the studies and their results in a book. I originally intended to include only the studies done in eastern North American forests (since the western forests have been the focus of other books), and although the focus here remains on eastern forests, I soon realized that including a global perspective added depth to the evidence.

Over and over I have read or heard espoused that "forests must be managed to be healthy." Perhaps forests must be managed to get the healthiest economic return, but true biological health is found in the unmanaged old-growth forests. I can say that because the scientists who have done these careful studies have offered their data to us. I also know it to be true because I have spent time in many, many old-growth forests and have heard the birdsong, witnessed the soaring canopies, and breathed the forest air.

"When we try to pick out anything by itself," John Muir wrote in *My First Summer in the Sierra*, "we find it hitched to everything else in the Universe." The truth of this often-quoted line will be evidenced over and over again in these pages. Although each chapter has a specific topic, you will soon see that they are all, indeed, hitched together.

Sources on page 195.

Acknowledgments

My deepest thanks go to the generous and patient consultants who have given their time to guide my efforts. I list them here in order of the chapters they are associated with:

The History of Forests—William Stein, Binghamton University, New York

The Oldest Trees—Neil Pederson, Eastern Kentucky University

The Largest Trees—Robert Leverett and Will Blozan, Eastern Native Tree Society

Amphibians—Stephen Tilley, Smith College

Snails—Daniel Douglas, Roane State Community College

Insects—Tim Schowalter, Louisiana State University Agricultural Center

Herbaceous Plants—Albert Meier, Western Kentucky University

Mosses—Gregory McGee, SUNY College of Environmental Science and Forestry, Syracuse

Fungi—Timothy Baroni, State University of New York at Cortland

Lichens—Steven Selva, University of Maine at Fort Kent; and Eric Peterson, California Academy of Sciences

Worms—Tami Ransom, Salisbury University

Mammals—Carolyn Mahan, Penn State Altoona; and Aaron Hogue, Salisbury University

Acknowledgments from the 2016 edition

This book began with the vision of collecting and publishing papers from various contributors. In response to my request for manuscripts, a number of people generously contributed original papers: Marc Abrams, Timothy Baroni, Daniel Douglas, Robert Leverett, Carolyn Mahan, Tim Schowalter, Steven Selva, and Stephen Tilley. The style and scope of the book changed over time, but those papers were critically helpful. Any errors or opinions in these pages are completely mine, but many of the useful facts came from the others.

In 2014 I was awarded the Mary Byrd Davis Residency, which allowed me to spend a month working on this book at the Bordeneuve Retreat in the French Pyrenees. Retreat owner Noelle Thompson made sure I could write all day ensconced in divine solitude and be rewarded at day's end with her marvelous food, wine, and companionship. Such a generous gift, and so personally meaningful, because the residency was endowed by Noelle's uncle, Robert Davis. Bob, as I know him, was husband to the late Mary Byrd Davis, who edited *Eastern Old-Growth Forests: Prospects for Rediscovery and Recovery* (1996) and *Old Growth in the East: A Survey* (2002). These publications are always within reach on my desk, and they have guided my work so often that I feel that this book is an extension of them. Her son, John Davis, has become a good friend. Together we continue speaking for the old-growth forests.

Concerned that old-growth forests are still falling, and inspired by the idea that we might allow "future old-growth forests" to recover, I created the Old-Growth Forest Network, a nonprofit organization. Deepest thanks to my board of directors for encouraging me to take time away from my executive director duties to complete this book. Particular thanks to Will Cook for assistance with editing. Thanks, also, to my loyal administrative assistant, Susan Barnett, for keeping the organization humming along while I was busy writing. Please visit our website, old-growthforest.net, to learn more about what we do. And a huge thanks to all the supporters of the Network. We are not just a network of forests—we are also a network of people who care about forests.

Finally, I wish to thank my extended tribe of family and friends—so many that I could not possibly name them all here. But if I had to pluck out a few names, I would extend special thanks to my daughter, Alyssa Maloof, who is the light of my life; to friend Tim Thompson, for keeping my beloved cat company during my long and frequent absences; and to Jamie Phillips for his companionship these past few years.

Acknowledgments for the 2023 edition

I thank those listed above for their continued support and encouragement. I belatedly thank my editors of the 2016 edition from Timber Press: Eve Goodman and Lorraine Anderson. I am grateful to Robert Kirk, at Princeton University Press, who believed that this book was important enough to update and keep in print. Jim Lutz and an anonymous reviewer took the time to carefully comment on the manuscript, and I thank them for that. A huge thank you to everyone at the Old-Growth Forest Network for creating an organization we can be proud of—one that is truly "speaking for the trees." The old forests are still in danger around the world. I thank everyone who is doing their best to save what's left and help some to recover.

Nature's Temples

I

What Is an Old-Growth Forest?

What is an old-growth forest? It is difficult to generalize about forests since each is different from every other in climate, in soils, in species, in its history. Trying to describe a typical old-growth forest is like trying to describe a typical human—exceptions can be found to anything you might say. Still, though, for that proverbial person from another planet, we might make an attempt. So here goes.

Old growth is a stage in a forest's development, but one that not all forests reach. In order to reach old growth, a forest must have escaped destruction for a long enough period of time to allow natural biological and ecosystem functions to be the dominant influence. In other words, there is a continuity that has allowed generations of trees (and other organisms) to come and go. These forests are sometimes called virgin or original or primary. In most of North America, old-growth forests were once the predominant land cover, and the place where the evolution of many species and their ecological interactions occurred. In just a few hundred years of commercial exploitation, we have reduced those former nature-ruled expanses to small isolated remnants. But those remnants still serve as examples, and they still have lessons to teach.

In the forests that have escaped clearing, some trees are able to reach their maximum life span. So the oldest trees are found in old-growth forests, or in marginal areas like cliff edges and wetlands that were difficult to log. A later chapter will discuss just what the maximum ages are for various species, but as one example, researchers near the Great Lakes found that half of the canopy trees in an old-growth forest there were two hundred or more years old. In an old-growth coastal redwood forest in California, the age of some canopy trees can be counted in thousands of years instead of hundreds. The advanced age of some of the trees in an old-growth forest is important because trees change structurally with age. The most obvious change is in size. Although age and size do not always track side by side, to a point the older trees are the larger trees. Wider branches in the canopy can support more life forms: more birds, more mosses, more mammals. Large limbs and wide trunks that develop hollows provide the structural diversity important to many organisms. The remnant old-growth forests generally contain the tallest trees, too. In the Eastern US, think Cook Forest in Pennsylvania or Congaree National Park in South Carolina; in the West, think Redwood National and State Parks in California. These unlogged forests demonstrate not only how many years various tree species can survive but also how large they can get.

Although the trees in an old-growth forest are older and larger, fewer trees grow there than in a younger forest. One reason for this is that most of the light is captured by the tall canopy trees. Younger trees in the understory must wait, almost in a suspended state, for their turn in the spotlight when they might get the extra sunlight they need and finally make it to the canopy. If too many decades go by without the needed light, the younger trees may die. But if one of the ancients dies first, the large area that its canopy formerly occupied is now flooded with light, as if a massive sunroof had just been installed. In this gap even herbaceous plants that need full sun can thrive. Younger trees race to fill the canopy space. All nearby trees, even the oldest, shift their growth slowly in response to the change. From a godlike height the canopy no longer looks uniform. Like a tooth missing from a child's mouth, the fallen tree has created a gap that results in an uneven canopy. In terms of biodiversity, the gaps are as important as the ancient canopy. They allow sunlight in.

Dead trees either remain standing or fall over. If they remain standing, they are called snags. Large snags, with their rotting wood and hollow spaces, create structural variation that can benefit many species, from the smallest insects to the largest mammals. A fallen tree, likewise, creates structural diversity. The trunk as it rots helps to create new moisture-holding soil. It is a bonanza for soil-dwelling fungi that mine it for nutrients that they then pass along to the living trees. The woody debris is also important habitat for forest-dwelling beetles and the organisms that feed on them. If the tree brought its roots along as it tipped over, the roots and the soil clinging to them create a mound that increases the structural diversity of the forest floor. Organisms that need standing water, such as frogs, benefit from the depressions; and organisms that need bare, well-drained soil, such as yellow birch seedlings, benefit from the mounds. The larger a tree is when it falls over, the larger these topographic variations are.

Piecing together this description, we can begin to get a picture of what a "typical" old-growth forest might look like. Our old-growth forest is likely to have large-diameter trees. If it is a multispecies forest, you will likely find large individuals of different species near each other. The bark on the old trees will look different from the bark on the younger trees of the same species. The forest also has tall trees and trees twisted by age. The crowns of the trees may exhibit short, angled limbs, almost antler-like, since they have faced centuries of environmental assaults. The forest has an overstory canopy layer, with trees of varying ages beneath the canopy. It has wood from dead trees—both standing and lying on the ground. There are gaps in the canopy, and growing beneath the gaps are plants that need the full sun that results from a disturbance. The ground is likely to have pits and mounds from long-ago tree falls. Someone who has visited many old-growth forests begins to develop an eye for these indicators. You will learn in these pages that in addition to these apparent structural differences, many biological differences between younger and older forests exist that are difficult to discern at a glance. Other lines of evidence, such as tree ring counts or historical photographs, may be used to corroborate the conclusion that this is, indeed, an old-growth forest.

If you are fortunate enough to experience such a forest, it is important to take every step necessary to ensure that it is recognized and protected. Although timber management and harvesting are important economically, most foresters agree that our remaining old-growth forests should be preserved. They are living examples of how our forests behave when they are unmanaged, and they give us a baseline against which to compare how biodiversity changes when we do manage forests. Preservation does not mean that the forest will always stay standing or always maintain the same species composition. Forests are constantly, if slowly, changing. Preservation means that we simply allow the forest to change at its own pace. Just because a forest was once destroyed—whether by humans or by natural events—does not mean it is unworthy of preservation.

Our old-growth remnants are so rare that we should not be content with merely preserving what remains. We still have an opportunity to set aside second-growth forests (ones that were formerly logged but are now growing back) for recovery. When I speak out for preservation of some of these middle-aged parcels, I occasionally hear that they are not old growth and are therefore nothing special. Do not forget that these future old-growth forests are exactly where hope for recovery exists. They may not be old growth again in our lifetimes, but we can leave them as our gift to the future. As Mary Byrd Davis wrote in her preface to *Eastern Old-Growth Forests*, "We are between two forested worlds—the natural forest of pre-settlement North America and the recovered forest of the future. . . . The earlier forested world is not dead. We are studying and struggling to preserve its living remnants. And we do not believe that the future forest is powerless to be born. These remnants—with our help—will become the seeds from which a renewed forest spreads."

Sources on page 195.

2

The History of Forests

I have been traveling all around the United States, giving talks about why we should be preserving some of our old-growth forests. When some ecologists and foresters hear me speak of saving these special places, they think that perhaps I have the mistaken notion that these forests can be frozen in time, never to change, like some sort of tree museum. I know better.

Change and change and change again is the story of our forests. This change cannot be stopped, nor would I want to stop it. The forces that shape each forest are themselves continually changing. For instance, climate patterns change, and the individual species in a forest change in response. A change may be beneficial for one species but detrimental to another. The shifts happen so slowly that they are usually imperceptible on a human time scale. But our long-term data sets tell us that the climate is getting hotter, drier, and we are experiencing more extreme weather events. This slow-motion dance of nature has many participants, each with their own unique choreography, and the dance we are witnessing now may be an entirely new one. We are really just starting to understand what is happening, yet at any point in time we can experience the results of all the varied forces in the forest we are walking through and gazing upon.

My mission is to honor what we have right *now*, right *here*, and to allow for the possibility of change. Only living, breathing earth ecosystems can produce new species of trees. Other ways we use—abuse—the land do not allow for a pulsing new forest type to arise. Farm fields, mowed lawns, parking lots, and roads do not allow for the possibility of change—of new, of perhaps better.

Let's take a long view of these changes. Forests did not always exist on this planet. In fact, there was not always life on this planet. On this remarkable rock that coalesced and cooled about 4.5 *billion* years ago, it took a billion years or so before the thing we call life appeared. We still have no idea exactly how that happened. At first life was small and simple, with no true distinction between what we now call plant and animal. Then those small living things became larger and larger and more and more different from each other until there were plants and animals. But only in the sea, nothing yet on land. Land organisms took a few billion more years to show up. The first low-growing plantlike organisms that moved from the edge of the sea up onto the mudflats inhabited a very empty and quiet place. There were no birds or insects to announce dusk and dawn. The blowing of the wind or the splattering of the rain would have been the only sounds. No trees yet, of course. No humans, no dinosaurs.

In this early safe space on the land—where nibbling water creatures could not reach them—the plants evolved to become larger and larger and larger, competing with each other for the sun's light.

If you want to define a tree as a plant that towers over your head, the first trees had fernlike leaves with woody stems. We now give them Latin names based on their fossils, but then, of course, they had no names. For 60 *million* years (from 383 to 323 million years ago), these first trees were found all over the earth. They were hugely abundant, especially in wet areas. The planet was much warmer and wetter then, and those early trees occupied a niche that would resemble something like the habitat of our modern-day mangroves.

The continents were in very different positions then, too. The land we now call the Catskills, in the state of New York, was south of the equator, and the early trees grew abundantly there. We know that because fossils of these ancient, early trees are found near the small town of Gilboa, New York. Gilboa has become world famous among paleontologists for having the oldest fossil forest on earth.

When I learned about the fossil forest, I wanted to go there and wander through the stony remains, to imagine myself in the first forest on earth, perhaps the first forest in the entire cosmos. For better or for worse, however, it had been covered over by backfill in a quarry. Better, researcher William Stein feels, because the site is now protected for some distant future generation that might have more sophisticated research methods; but worse, because dreamers like myself cannot see the fossils in situ but must be satisfied with the fossilized stumps placed here and there throughout town, such as the ones near Gilboa's town hall.

For a short time in 2010, though, the quarry backfill was removed, and Stein and others got to work mapping, collecting, and documenting. The map they created at least lets me wander that early forest in my mind. It was a wetland forest of just three species: a dominant tree species, a long vine-like plant with fronds, and one club moss–type plant. There would have been no insects or other animals in this forest. No pollinators, since there were no flowering plants yet. All these species reproduced by spores, so reproduction was dependent upon a moist environment.

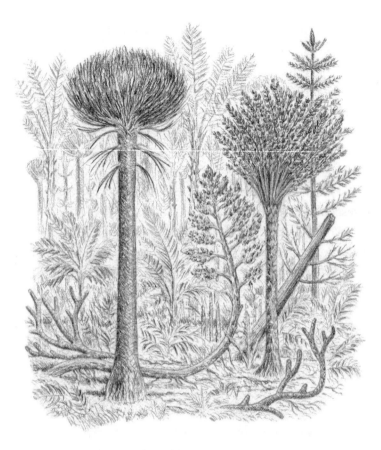

An artistic representation, based on fossil evidence, of what the earth's first forests looked like.

On this ancient, warm-wet earth, coastal trees became wildly successful and were found on every continent, covering vast acreages. The wheel of evolution was spinning out new tree species and, eventually, animals that crawled among them. (One of the first was a gigantic scorpion-like creature.) After *tens of millions* of years, trees at last broke their bondage from moist environments by developing their embryos in a weatherproof package we now call a seed. With this newly evolved structure, trees could cover both the wet and the dry land areas. Tree roots spread out through cracks in the rocks, and leaves fell to the ground. Soil was being created.

All of this vegetation was sucking the carbon out of the sky. And plants were speeding the erosion of rocks by increasing the size of the cracks. The soil created by fallen plant fragments also caused chemical weathering of rocks, which removed even more carbon from the atmosphere. The climate changed, but not like today when carbon dioxide is increasing and the globe is warming. Instead, the opposite was happening: carbon dioxide was decreasing and the planet was cooling. Glaciers formed. An ice age was on its way. This ice age, possibly caused by the trees, wound up driving 70 percent of the species on earth to extinction. It was a long, pulsing decline over *millions* of years. The oceans were particularly hard hit, and coral reefs died out. Ironically, some of the tree species that may have caused the ice age became victims themselves. None of the tree species that existed then still grow naturally in North America.

I wonder if there is a lesson here. We see today's changes in the atmosphere and hang our heads in shame. *If only* we could stop driving so much, *if only* we could get our act together regarding renewable energy, *if only* we weren't such flawed creatures. We tend to think of trees as good, or at least benign; but if we cast blame for changing the earth's climate back then, trees may have been the culprits. But they did it with no feelings of guilt:

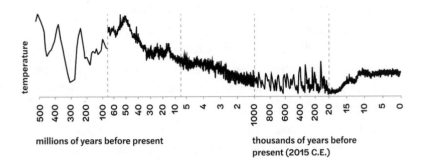

millions of years before present   **thousands of years before present (2015 C.E.)**

A long view of how average temperatures have changed on planet Earth (Anna Eshelman, based on a graph created by Glen Fergus). Note that 50 million years ago the planet was warmer than it is today.

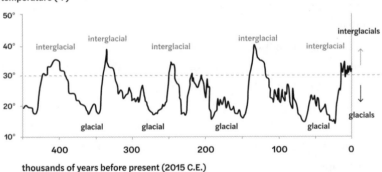

thousands of years before present (2015 C.E.)

An expansion of the right side of the previous graph, showing the cycle of glacial and interglacial periods over the past 450 thousand years.

they were just doing what trees do. Should we have called that era the Silvicene?

Many, many species disappeared from the earth then, but the one thing that never disappeared was the drive of evolution. New species arose, and the new species were even more successful in covering the planet than the former ones. Then another great extinction. Then another recovery. On and on. Change after change, sometimes separated by *hundreds of millions* of years, and sometimes by only *tens of millions* of years. *Only* tens of millions of years? Ha! When I stand next to a tree that is four hundred years old, it stretches my imagination to picture that seed germinating so long ago. To try to extend that thought to 4,000 years ago (and we do have such trees living on earth) seems near impossible. Now keep going: How about 40,000 years ago (when human beings as we know them first appeared)? Can you hold such a long passage of time in your imagination? I can't. So how can any of us manage to understand a *million* years, let alone *tens of millions* of years? And yet the forests have been growing and evolving for much longer than that.

Now consider our forest 50 million years ago. The planet had warmed considerably by then—in fact, it was much warmer than it is now. At that time the landmass we call North America had a mixed evergreen and broad-leaved forest stretching continuously across the middle of the northern latitudes. Most of the tree species we are familiar with today were part of that forest, including fir, spruce, pine, maple, hemlock, beech, walnut, and elm. But the climate didn't keep still—it never keeps still—and changes in temperature and precipitation eventually fragmented the forest. The land on the eastern side of the Rocky Mountains became drier, and much of the forest disappeared. Many of the broad-leaved tree species died out from the western Pacific forests too, but the coniferous forest remained intact. How astonishing that when I visit an old-growth redwood forest in California, I am visiting a place that may have been forested continually for 50 million years!

Now fast-forward again to the scale of "only" *hundreds of thousands* of years. The roller coaster of cooling/warming/cooling/warming has continued. Glaciers have grown and shrunk and grown and shrunk again. We happen to be in a warming period now; our last glacial period gave way to an interglacial period 18,000 years ago.

The forest I feel most connected to, the eastern temperate deciduous forest, has only been in place, roughly as it is, for about ten thousand years. Many of the states where I now hike among pine trees, beech trees, hemlocks, and maples (think New York, Pennsylvania, Massachusetts) were under glacial ice 18,000 years ago. The states farther south, where I hike among oaks, hickories, and maples, were coniferous forests of pine, spruce, and fir during those glacial times. Some areas were so cold they couldn't support forests at all, and the sand blew across the landscape into great dunes. But then the climate warmed again, and the glaciers retreated.

In the southeastern United States, some pockets of forest stayed reasonably protected from the glaciers and the cold (think Tennessee and North Carolina). In those special coves, some of the tender plant species survived our most recent ice age. When the climate warmed again, they could expand out of the sheltered coves and across the landscape. The cold-loving conifers hung on for a while, but in some places they were outcompeted by the aggressive, warmth-loving deciduous trees.

What we have today is a fascinating and complicated mix of trees that were around before the glaciers, trees that moved south as the glaciers covered their former territory, and trees that somehow survived and then moved north as the glaciers retreated. Now braid into that forest history whether the soils in a place are wet or dry, rocky or rich, acidic or alkaline, and you get a palette of green and brown that could fascinate forever. Far from boring.

Sometimes this long view brings a more peaceful perspective. When I give talks about the condition of our planet's forests today, it seems that someone always wants to bring up a current threat—some insect or fungus that threatens to bring a horrible, irreversible change to our forests. A partial current list includes oak wilt, beech bark disease, pine bark beetle, emerald ash borer, and hemlock woolly adelgid. Looking closely, these do seem tragic, but when one steps back a bit it is possible to see that not only do these insects and diseases come and go, but tree species themselves come and go. Beyond these comings and goings we have had forests on planet Earth for *hundreds of millions* of years. The tragedy to me is that we are now occupying so much possible forestland with concrete and asphalt and crops and cars and homes and mines and impoundments and the like that the ever-changing forest has fewer places in which to become what it will be next. Imagine if those few southern cove forests had been turned into monocultures or shopping malls before the glacial age. We would still have forests today, but they would be very, very different. May there always be refuges.

Sources on pages 195–96.

3

The Oldest Trees

A friend recently told me this true story from the town where he grew up. In a farmer's field near the main road in town grew a huge and beautiful white oak tree. The trunk tapered smoothly up from the base, narrowed in the center, and then flared out into a wide, perfectly symmetrical canopy. Very few people actually went up and touched the tree, but when they drove by it (for many people that was twice a day) they would look at the tree and appreciate its presence. They imagined that it would take at least four people with arms outstretched to circle the whole tree. It occupied perhaps a quarter of an acre of land. It had to be many hundreds of years old, they thought. Then one year the unthinkable happened—the tree fell over in a storm. This time people parked their cars and walked up to visit the fallen tree. Someone suggested counting the rings. They found that the tree was only ninety-five years old!

In this book I have separated the discussion of tree age from tree size, but ecologically, trees that are both large *and* old have a unique and important role to play. Unfortunately, on a global scale, populations of large old trees are declining. In the same way that large-bodied animals such as elephants and whales are now threatened, large old trees are also imperiled. In ecosystems subject to intensive industrial forestry, little or no intent exists to provide a continuous supply of large old trees.

Just because a tree is very large does not mean it is very old, and just because it is very old does not mean it is very large. Take a look at the drawing (copied to scale from a photograph) of a man standing next to a 326-year-old northern red oak, the oldest one of its species ever documented. I look at that and think, meh, nice, but I could show you a few larger in my town. You may have one larger than it in your backyard.

Speaking of backyards, imagine growing up next to an old-growth forest. Tom Howard grew up next to the seven-acre Wizard of Oz Memorial Oak Grove in North Syracuse, New York. The biggest red oak tree there is impressively large, but it is "only" 142 years old. Meanwhile, Jack Ruddat, who studied the old-growth forests in Connecticut, aged trees by coring them and found a hemlock tree less than two inches in diameter that was 144 years old. And another hemlock in Connecticut, narrower than the width of my outstretched hand, was 212 years old! This illustrates the point that age and size are somewhat independent. Growing conditions are the most important determinant of size.

The best way to judge a tree's age is not by hugging it but by looking up. The oldest trees are often very tall, having reached for the top of the canopy over many years. Relative height seems to be a better indicator of age than relative girth—but exceptions abound in the forest, as elsewhere.

A tall old tree generally has greater trunk volume compared to branch volume. A closer look at the trunk shape may reveal a gentle waviness (called sinuosity). To my eye, however, it is the architecture of the branches that tells which trees are truly ancient. Look for tall trees that have fewer limbs, and limbs

Man standing next to a 326-year-old northern red oak in Massachusetts.

Man standing next to a 142-year-old northern red oak in New York. The much smaller white oak in pieces on the ground to the right was 198 years old when it fell.

that are thick and twisting. Instead of throwing main limbs upward, wide, and open, as some beautiful middle-aged oaks do, an ancient tree has at least a few limbs that are strangely shaped. Look for a limb that comes thickly out of the trunk and then makes an unexpected turn. A little further on it may make another turn, and then something seems to have happened to the outermost part of the branch; it is dead. A branch on the other side of the tree may have a strange shape, too. It takes a quick turn and then divides into two branches; one of the branches aims straight upward, while the other goes out at a 90-degree angle. Then this outward branch takes a wiggle, and another wiggle, and as you follow it closely, isolating just this branch, another and another. Strange. Although the tree may be a bit taller than the others nearby, overall it seems narrower. When you see trees

Growth form of an old tree.

shaped like that, you know you are walking among the ancients. You could be looking at a three-hundred-year-old tree. This tree has, dynamically, albeit slowly, responded to changes in the forest over centuries.

Another key indicator to look for is how tree bark changes with the age of the tree. As trees age from youth to maturity, the bark tends to get thicker and sometimes shaggier. But on the very oldest trees of some species, the bark then thins out again (called balding).

My description is idealized, of course, and wide variation exists in the way different trees age. The twisting and turning and balding I describe is much like the wrinkling, scarring, and bentness that occurs in our bodies as we age. A long life gives the opportunity for long exposure to the elements and to the chance events that change us. Genetics count too, but we can't get old without looking it, and neither can trees.

Indigenous people probably noticed these differences among trees, but these days the differences must be pointed out before most people notice them. Neil Pederson, an expert on aging trees, had permission to core just twenty trees at the 346-acre Floracliff Nature Preserve in Kentucky. But which twenty trees should that be? He taught the preserve manager the characteristics to look for and then returned later to core the trees the manager had selected. It turned out that all of the trees were more than 250 years old and half were more than 300 years old, evidence that Pederson is a great teacher, the manager was a great pupil, *and* that the forest was ancient.

In the western parts of North America, where trees can live for thousands of years, the effects of time are even more dramatic. The tallest spire on a tree is frequently dead due to desiccation from reaching above the surrounding canopy or lightning strikes that are drawn to the tallest points above the ground. A new leading shoot may take over when that happens, but after eighty years or so that leader may succumb and another may form, and another. The result is a candelabra-like crown. In these extremely ancient trees, the crevices and cracks accumulate enough soil to enable other tree seeds to germinate and grow, and the result is fascinatingly complex. It is not unusual at all to see a hundred-year-old tree growing out of a thousand-year-old tree. I have also

Tree bark changes with age. Some species, like maples and hemlocks, get shaggier, and some species, like tulip poplars and black gums, get smoother. This swamp white oak's bark is balding near the bottom of the trunk.

Candelabra form of an ancient western red cedar
(based on a photo by Roger Barnett).

noticed that the very oldest *and* very largest (think coastal red-woods and giant sequoias) tend to sag at the ankles the way an old person might. Wavy rolls near the base show the weight these trees have been holding up for many centuries.

The oldest of the old—the Great Basin bristlecone pines of the Sierra Nevada range in California, the oldest trees on the planet—show sinuosity and the candelabra effects, but they are not extremely large. If you were looking for the oldest of trees and you equated large with old, you would walk right by them. They are small because their environment is harsh: dry, windy, high altitude. But they also live so long because of this environment: not many tree-boring insects or tree-rotting fungi can live there, and if they did it would be difficult for them to penetrate the extremely dense, slow-growing wood. Not many human neighbors sacrificing trees to clear their viewshed there either. Some of these trees were already thousands of years old when Jesus was born in that manger.

Sometimes, though, the largest trees are the oldest. I am thinking of a certain tree I came across in the swamps of the Eastern Shore of Maryland. I was searching for old forests when I came across a massive trunk. Whoa! The lowest branches were so far from the ground that at first I couldn't tell what the tree was. The bark looked like nothing I had seen before; it was thin and mossy. Slowly it all came together. I was looking at a black gum like no black gum I had ever seen. It dwarfed the maples, oaks, and bald cypress trees all around it. I knew right away it was a champion—either local, or state, or national. And I knew it was old, very old, perhaps four hundred years old. But I had no desire to core a tree like that to find out for certain. She (not an *it* anymore) was in a protected forest owned by the Nature Conservancy, and I did not want to cause any trauma that might tip her over the edge to decline. (Would you suggest piercing your hundred-year-old grandmother's navel?)

Black gum can live to be more than six hundred years old! Only indigenous people lived here when the seed she grew from fell and germinated in a landscape that was 95 percent forested. That small forest margin remained uncut until the present because it was too wet for other uses. And that tree remained standing because it was not a popular species for building or burning. No, I would not want to pierce her.

But someone has. I have shown the exact location of the tree to only a few people. Someone I showed the tree to showed it to someone else, and that someone else had the tools required for coring, and the curiosity, but not the restraint. No age could be determined because her core had some hollowness—not unusual in a tree that old. It remains to be seen if the coring will have any negative effects.

My hesitation about coring is not shared by all tree people. Many foresters and other researchers have been taught that coring does not harm a tree. Although the wound from coring never heals, the tree walls it off (called compartmentalization). For vigorously growing young trees, or resinous-sap–producing trees, this may not be a problem. I am not against all coring, just as I am not against all logging. There is just a time and a place where it should be done, and a time and a place where it should not.

Look what happened to the oldest tree we know of, one of those Great Basin bristlecone pines: a graduate student trying to age the tree got his expensive corer stuck in the dense wood. The ranger, who helped him out by cutting the tree to release the corer, didn't know it was the oldest tree on earth when he cut it down. He was not a bad person. The person who cored the black gum is not a bad person either; I happen to like him very much, and I have helped him core other trees. And there are yet other places where I wish he would do some coring—like the old-growth forest in the heart of town slated for destruction. Unquestionable evidence of the trees' advanced age might help us save them.

Another example of "coring for good" comes from Stadium Woods. This small forest is on the campus of Virginia Tech, in Blacksburg. The forestry, biology, and ecology faculty knew that the forest was old, but they didn't know *how old* until the campus administration announced that the forest would be removed to create space for a new building. That threat got university faculty studying and coring the trees. When many of the oak trees were found to be older than the United States (pre-1776), the faculty's reasons for wanting to preserve the forest were substantiated and forest lovers all over the nation got involved. To me this was a beneficial use of coring, and arguably worth the risk of damage since the trees were threatened anyway. (As of this writing, the forest will not be cleared for construction, but the university has put no permanent protections in place for the rare remnant.)

Another argument for coring, beyond just where it is useful for forest preservation, is that coring can help us understand forest histories. We are just now learning from core samples about the maximum ages possible for our tree species. For instance, in 2019, Dave Stahle and colleagues found a stand of very old bald cypress (*Taxodium distichum*) in the Black River of North Carolina. Coring enabled us to learn that at least one of these trees was a thousand years older than our previous maximum known age for this species! (Yes, of course I have been to see those trees.) Neil Pederson has done a great service by keeping the information on maximum eastern tree ages up to date and freely accessible on the Eastern OLDLIST website at ldeo.columbia. edu/~adk/oldlisteast/.

A similar list is kept for ancient trees across the globe by Rocky Mountain Tree-Ring Research at rmtrr.org/oldlist.htm. That list shows that a Great Basin bristlecone pine in California is the oldest known living tree species on earth, at 4,850 years. Giant sequoias can live to be over 3,000 years old, but none of the trees documented to be that old are still living. Some of the

Table 1. Maximum ages of trees of the eastern United States, from data shared by Neil Pederson and others

Species	Maximum age
Bald cypress (*Taxodium distichum*)	2,624
Northern white-cedar (*Thuja occidentalis*)	1,051
Eastern red cedar (*Juniperus virginiana*)	940
Black gum (*Nyssa sylvatica*)	679
Eastern hemlock (*Tsuga canadensis*)	555
Tulip poplar (*Liriodendron tulipifera*)	509
White oak (*Quercus alba*)	464
Long-leaf pine (*Pinus palustris*)	458
Chestnut oak (*Quercus montana*)	427
Pond cypress (*Taxodium ascendens*)	417
American sycamore (*Platanus occidentalis*)	412
Yellow buckeye (*Aesculus flava*)	410
Pitch pine (*Pinus rigida*)	398
Yellow birch (*Betula alleghaniensis*)	367
Sweet birch (*Betula lenta*)	361
Shagbark hickory (*Carya ovata*)	354
Cucumber tree (*Magnolia acuminata*)	348
Northern red oak (*Quercus rubra*)	326
Pignut hickory (*Carya glabra*)	325
Shortleaf pine (*Pinus echinata*)	324
Sugar maple (*Acer saccharum*)	315
Carolina hemlock (*Tsuga caroliniana*)	307
Red maple (*Acer rubrum*)	300

western junipers and pines live for more than a thousand years, but they tend to live in windswept places, and they are fairly small and gnarled. I'm sure hikers pass by them all the time without appreciating their longevity.

In 2021, after I spoke out to try to save a hundred-year-old forest on state land, a journalist reached out to the forest manager for a comment. The manager said that if we don't cut the trees they are just going to fall down and die (or die and then fall down). This is a scare tactic I have heard used on private forest owners, too. The implied threat is that after a certain age the forest will "collapse" and lose its monetary value. The truth is that both young and old trees die in old-growth forests. But unlike what you may hear from someone suggesting you cut now, average mortality rates are lower in the old-growth forests. In one study, tree mortality in young forest plots was 4.42 percent, while mortality in old-growth plots was 0.60 percent; meaning that young trees died at seven times the rate of old trees. Some of the trees taken because they were "just going to die" had the potential to live for hundreds of years more—into an era where you and I and the forest manager are likely to have been forgotten.

Sources on page 196.

4

Birds in the Forest

The birds that come to our backyard feeders—the cardinals, sparrows, blue jays, and finches—are not the ones that need old-growth forests. The ones that need the ancient forest are the cavity dwellers and the ground nesters, like brown creepers, red-breasted nuthatches, and yellow-bellied flycatchers. These birds feed mostly on live insects instead of seeds. You may not be as familiar with them.

In North America the populations of more than half of our bird species are declining. We have lost 29 percent of our birds since 1970. Part of this loss is connected to pesticide use in areas that are used by grassland birds, but another part of the loss is due to the way our forests are managed. Forest stands that are older, more mixed, and more structurally diverse support a greater number and a greater richness of birds. Our feathered friends are so varied in their habitat preferences that it is impossible to generalize about what effect forest management has on them; instead, one must look at each particular species to see if that species does best in an old forest, a young forest, or no forest at all.

Some bird species prefer forest interiors, some species prefer forest edges, and some species prefer clear-cuts. As a forest progresses through time from clear-cut to mature, the species found there change. In terms of the number of species only, sometimes more species are found in the younger forests than in the old growth. But the species that *are* found in the old growth often have trouble surviving in younger forests. Some of the old-growth specialists are cavity nesters—and cavities are more likely to be found in old forests with large trees containing rotten wood. The birds that do better in old growth also tend to forage for insects in the canopy and on the trunks. Larger, older trees equals larger canopies and trunks, which equals more insects, particularly mites and spiders. Forest management may affect a bird's food supply and nesting choices more than it directly affects the bird.

Size matters too, since the larger the forest, the more plant diversity it contains, and the more plant diversity, the higher the insect diversity and the greater the insect populations, and the greater the insect populations, the more birds the forest can support. Ovenbirds and Kentucky warblers nest more densely in larger forests, and worm-eating warblers do not even nest in a forest unless it is larger than 8,000 square feet. Evening grosbeak, a species in decline, has been found to be sensitive to patch size. The endangered red-cockaded woodpecker requires as much as 500 acres to be successful. Again, the bigger the forest, the better.

The Alberta Biodiversity Monitoring Institute lists thirty-seven Alberta resident bird species that are old-growth dependent, but they define old growth as anything more than eighty years old. In a northern Minnesota study, thirty-five bird species were observed in either wilderness forests or managed forests. Species richness and total number of species were higher in the unmanaged wilderness forests, although two species were significantly more abundant in the managed forests (mourning warbler and chipping sparrow). Eight species were significantly more abundant in the wilderness forests: black-capped chickadee, brown creeper, Canada warbler, golden-crowned kinglet, least flycatcher, red-breasted nuthatch, winter wren, and yellow-bellied flycatcher. Black-capped chickadee and red-breasted nuthatch are both cavity nesters that rely on rotten wood or pre-excavated cavities.

Brown creepers are an interesting example of how and why a bird might be considered old-growth dependent. The creepers eat mainly insects and spiders that they find on the trunks of trees. Large trees with deep bark furrows and snags with diverse decaying surfaces are both more common in old-growth forests, and they also support a greater abundance of insects and spiders, so it is no surprise that the brown creeper is more abundant in old-growth forests. But in addition to offering the right food sources, old-growth forests have the right nesting areas for the brown creeper, who builds a hammock-like nest under the flaking bark of large snags. In Alaska, when old spruce trees were removed by logging after they were killed by bark beetles, brown creeper populations declined. The dead trees would have provided good nesting and foraging sites.

For all these reasons, one team of scientists writes: "The reliance of the brown creeper on specific forest structures characteristic of mature forest suggests that low-intensity harvest does not provide suitable habitat, and reserves of unharvested forest should be maintained for brown creeper conservation." Another team that studied the effect of forest management on the brown creeper found that even partial harvesting by single-tree selection caused a decline in breeding populations. They recommended that "patches of untreated forest should be maintained in managed forest landscapes at all times for this and other taxa requiring old forest conditions." They considered the brown creeper a good indicator species for old-growth forests.

In a British Columbia study done in Douglas fir forests,

Brown creeper, an indicator species for old-growth forests.

twelve bird species were found to be indicative of old growth. The reasons for their preference for that habitat differed by species. Birds associated with downed, coarse, woody debris were brown creepers, red-breasted nuthatches, chestnut-backed chickadees, and Pacific wrens. Birds associated with large trees and canopy gaps were olive-sided flycatchers and Pacific-slope flycatchers. Birds associated with high complexity in both the crown and the understory were golden-crowned kinglets, pine siskins, purple finches, and three warblers—Townsend's, yellow-rumped, and Wilson's. Another Canadian study, this one done in Ontario, found that black-throated green warblers and Blackburnian warblers were associated with "super-canopy" white pines more than ninety-eight feet tall.

When Christopher Haney analyzed Pennsylvania's breeding bird survey, he discovered that more than a third of the bird species were more likely to occur in old-growth conifer-hardwood forest than anywhere else in the entire state. This group contained some of Pennsylvania's rarest breeding birds, including yellow-bellied flycatcher and Swainson's thrush. Red-shouldered hawks and barred owls were more likely to be in found in the old-growth forests than anywhere else in the state. Even within the old-growth group, birds had habitat preferences. For instance, red-breasted nuthatches, brown creepers, winter wrens, and golden-crowned kinglets preferred conifers, while blue-headed vireos preferred hardwoods, and hairy woodpeckers preferred mixed forests with large snags and logs. Blackburnian warblers were most likely to be found in hemlock and white pine old-growth forests.

Yellow-bellied flycatchers are never found breeding in young, managed forests. These rare birds prefer swampy areas containing evergreen trees, some standing and some downed. Since the yellow-bellied flycatcher builds its nest on the ground, frequently under cinnamon ferns, the ideal nesting area offers

The winter wren, another bird that is more abundant in older forests.

a ground layer that is a combination of mosses and ferns, and dense shrubs such as blueberry, mountain laurel, and viburnum. This dense vegetation prevents nest predators, like blue jays and chipmunks, from locating the nests. It is the complex structure that develops over time in an old-growth forest that is so critical to this bird's success. We can try to mimic these environmental conditions with newer types of forest management, but so far we have not been successful in convincing the birds that new old growth is equivalent to the real thing.

Lately there has been a push from grants awarded by the US Fish and Wildlife Service to create "young forest" for a few select bird species like the golden-winged warbler and the ruffed grouse. Unfortunately, this young forest is often created by cutting down older forests on their way to recovery, instead of creating it "from scratch" by reclaiming open turf areas or powerline right of ways. The many species being negatively affected by this program—such as the birds that need old forests—are simply ignored. The cutting also fragments forests, allowing nest parasites like brown-headed cowbirds to destroy the nests of interior forest-dwelling birds. And a final blow is inflicted when the forest openings are invaded by non-native invasive plants that can preclude forest recovery. A reminder is needed here that in states where this is happening, like New Jersey, there are already many, many more acres of "young forests" than there are old-growth forests.

Recently the ivory-billed woodpecker was officially declared extinct. Its habitat was the old-growth bottomland forests of the southern US. That large and beautiful bird faced the double jeopardy of being popular to shoot at and being dependent on old-growth habitat. The director of the Cornell Lab of Ornithology is quoted as saying the bird's extinction is "a consequence of the fact that we cut down every last trace of the virgin forest of the Southeastern U.S. We took all that away." Well, there are little pockets left, but not enough, not enough.

Sources on pages 196–97.

5

Amphibians
in the Forest

What does it mean to call a forest *healthy*? That word, like *freedom*, evokes a positive feeling but has no firm definition. Words like that can easily be abused because anyone can use them any way they want. In the 1980s, Bruce Bury was inspired to test claims made by the forest industry that younger forests contained better wildlife habitat conditions than old-growth forests and that abundant wildlife populations inhabit logged lands. He was annoyed that the term *wildlife* had become synonymous with large game species. Any ecologist knows that the game species are just a minor part of woodland wildlife. What about the salamanders? They are wildlife, too. In fact they are a very abundant and widespread component of it. A study done in New Hampshire in the 1970s found that the weight of the salamanders per acre of forest was twice the weight of the mammals and the nesting birds in that same forest.

When most people think of habitat for amphibians (frogs and salamanders) they think of ponds, but a great many of these gentle and beautiful creatures actually spend the majority of their time on land in the forest. And even those that do need open water for breeding frequently depend on the temporary pools found in forests. These pools dry up in the summer after the trees leaf out and draw the water up to their leaves. As a result of their temporary nature, these ponds are free of fish—a perfect habitat for amphibian eggs to be laid and larvae to develop. Other amphibians do not need open water at all; they lay their eggs in the damp earth or in moist rotting logs.

Bury decided to focus on amphibians to test the claims of abundant wildlife in logged forests. He compared old-growth redwood sites in California with redwood sites logged between six and fifteen years previously. He found more individuals and greater biomass of all amphibians in the old-growth forests. In addition, he found a number of species that either were only found in the old-growth forests or were very strongly associated with them. Consider these five as indicator species for old growth in California: tailed frogs, Olympic torrent salamanders, Pacific giant salamanders, Ensatina salamanders, and slender salamanders. It is highly likely that these delightful species have been living in association with the western old-growth forests for millions of years.

If you are one of these five amphibians, a recently logged forest is not a healthy place for you. But why not? What is it about old-growth forests that these species need? Amphibians are all thin skinned and require a moist environment. They don't necessarily need a pond or a stream; many species live entirely ground-based lives, but the ground must be cool and damp, and crevices, root channels, or fissures must give them access to the cool, damp layers. Looking more specifically at the five indicator species, we know that the tailed frog needs clear, cold, fast streams. While most frogs lay their eggs and leave them, the female tailed frog harbors her fertilized eggs within her body; otherwise they would be swept downstream. She is seven years

An eastern red-backed salamander, a common woodland creature.

old before she reaches sexual maturity, and she may live up to fourteen years. Logging in her habitat could expose her stream to sun and silt, making it too warm for her or her offspring to survive. Likewise, the Olympic torrent salamander needs cold, clean water; springs bubbling up from the ground in a shady forest or the sprayed margins of a shady waterfall are both habitats that suit it. The other three salamanders on the list are all without lungs. They cannot take a breath. They get the oxygen they need and release their waste gases through their skin. But their skin must be moist for this trick to work. So dry equals dead for these and many other species of salamanders.

It is not really big old trees that these amphibians need so much as it is the habitat created within an old-growth forest with big old trees. The ancient forest creates a moist environment with smaller fluctuations in temperature and humidity. Logging, by

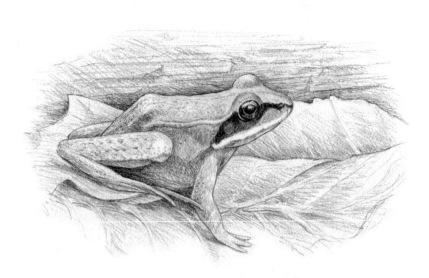

Wood frog, found in forests of the eastern United States.

contrast, increases the light reaching the ground, causing higher soil temperatures and resulting in faster drying of the forest floor. This could mean death for a lungless salamander, especially if the soil has been compacted by logging equipment and no underground alleys of refuge have been left intact.

Most of the research on old-growth forests, and old-growth-dependent amphibians in particular, has been done in the western United States, but a study was done on lungless salamanders in Missouri that compared old-growth (more than 120 years old), second-growth (70 to 80 years old), and regeneration-cut (less than 5 years old) forests. The researchers found mostly southern red-backed salamanders: an average of 488 salamanders per acre in the old-growth forests, 96 per acre in the second-growth forests, and zero in the regeneration-cut forests. Those numbers are hard to argue with.

One likely reason for the greater success of the salamanders in the old-growth forests is that these forests have larger logs on the forest floor, in later stages of decay. Big old decaying logs mean a damp environment protected from extremes in temperature, and more insects. Both shelter and food are available for the salamanders. It may seem strange to think of them this way, but salamanders can be imagined as the large carnivorous predators of the forest floor. Many insects, some quite tiny, are deadwood dependent, and these insects, in turn, may be fed on by woodland ground beetles. The salamanders in this forest-floor world might serve as the top predators, keeping the predator beetle populations in check. But they themselves might also become food—for an opossum or a ground-feeding bird.

The researchers in Missouri concluded: "Management activities based on commercial rotations could result in lower plethodontid densities due to lack of suitable habitat. Increasing the rotation length in managed forests would provide older, mature forests that play a critical role in maintaining relatively high densities of plethodontid salamanders."

The term *plethodontid* refers to a salamander in the genus *Plethodon*. If you live in the eastern United States and you head to the woods today, roll over a log, and find a salamander, chances are very, very good it will be a plethodontid—probably a red-backed salamander. Of the 380 species of lungless salamanders, 55 are in the genus *Plethodon*. None of them need open water, as all are completely terrestrial. If you survey salamanders in the northeastern United States, you will likely find a maximum of 5 species, but if you survey them in the southern Appalachians you could find as many as 25 different kinds. This difference in biodiversity is because the land that was once under glaciers is still in recovery, while the southern Appalachians had cove forest refuges where salamanders could survive the ice age, evolve into new species during their isolation, and then recolonize new habitat as the broad-leaved trees dispersed again. As a result of this history, our southeastern US forests have a greater diversity of amphibians than any other temperate forests on earth, and

The spotted salamander, which usually makes its home in a hardwood forest.

all terrestrial salamanders reach their peak populations in old-growth forests except for two exceedingly rare species found only on rocky outcrops.

Northern red-backed salamanders have a very interesting and well-studied social system. Like humans, they often form monogamous pairs. The females are more attracted to large males, males that have a prey-rich territory, and males that do not bear odors from other females. Females can discover how prey-rich a male's territory is by squashing his fecal pellets and seeing what he has been feeding on. Once a pair has formed, the male will punish the female if she has foraged with another male, which he can sense by detecting the other male's odor on her skin. Punishment takes the form of threat postures and nipping.

In one study comparing old-growth forests with variously disturbed forests in New York, researchers found that northern red-backed salamander populations had recovered sixty years after disturbance (unless the forests were converted to coniferous types); however, that study had very small sample numbers.

Although red-backed salamanders are still common, overall lungless salamander populations have declined, and we still don't know exactly why. Is it climate change, invasive earthworms, pathogens, or habitat loss? Or is it a combination of some or all of these? These organisms are in trouble, and we still don't fully understand the role they play in an ecosystem.

Hartwell Welsh and Sam Droege suggest that these salamanders might be the ideal organism for monitoring the health of a forest due to their abundance, longevity, site fidelity, small territory size, and sensitivity to air and water pollution. Also, because of their harmlessness and their location on the forest floor, they are relatively easy to sample. To some, a healthy forest might be defined as fast tree-growth rates and straight-grained wood for harvesting, but to researchers such as Welsh and Droege, salamanders are a better indicator of health since they reflect the forest's balance of other small organisms, leaf litter, moisture, acidity, and soil structure.

Sources on pages 197–98.

6

Snails in the Forest

When you love the forest ecosystem and speak out on its behalf, you may be asked to visit forests, speak to groups, and be on committees. This is how I found myself on the Citizens Advisory Committee of the Chesapeake and Pocomoke State Forests in Maryland. This committee was formed to comply with requirements for Forest Stewardship Certification (FSC) of the forests. The committee was supposed to include a dozen representatives: a degreed ecologist (me), a person involved with a wildlife organization, a person involved with tourism, a representative from a conservation organization, a student with natural resource interest from a local university, a local waterman, a representative from one of the local indigenous tribes, a local hunter, a person involved with a local recreational business, a timber products operator, a person employed by a local forest product industry, and a licensed forester associated with a private business interest. I was on the committee for almost ten years, and we met a few times a year. Most of the time no more than four people from the committee were present. I saw the tourism representative once, and the hunter a few times. I never saw the indigenous person or the waterman. The timber products operator (a logger) was at every meeting. A number of times we were the only two committee members present.

Our primary duty was to comment on the annual work plan that described the timber harvests scheduled for the coming year. I took my duties seriously, and I tried to personally visit the forests where final harvests were planned. One forest in particular concerned me; it was right next to a recreational trail, and it contained many mature trees, including white oaks, southern red oaks, hickories, loblolly pines, short-leaf pines, red maples, and black gums. It wasn't an old-growth forest, but it was older than most in the area. Understory trees included dogwood, holly, and serviceberry. The shrub layer included mountain laurel and blueberry.

Once a year when the FSC auditors came through, we would be invited to attend field audits to examine the forest management firsthand. One particular audit experience stayed with me vividly. We visited the forest of particular concern to me, which I had suggested removing from the work plan. The trucks had just left, and not a single tree had been left standing. To me it looked like death and devastation, but judging by the comments from the forest managers and the auditors, there was no problem. As we headed back to the van, I knew that I must represent the citizens and the organisms that couldn't do so themselves. I stepped onto a stump more than 2 feet wide and got everyone's attention.

"When I look at the forest surrounding this clear-cut, all I see are young pines. This forest was one of the oldest and most diverse in the area. You claim to be managing this state forest for a combination of mature pine and oak, but that is exactly what you just removed. A few weeks ago this was a seed- and insect-filled forest—ideal habitat for many birds and other animals. Where are those animals now? There were no invasive species at all in this

Carychium exile, the old-growth indicator snail.

forest. Will we be able to say the same thing ten years from now? Will the white oaks ever again get as large as this one at my feet?" (It was close to a hundred years old.) My stump speech was over, no one said a word, and we continued our walk back to the van.

Later, I thought I should have asked them if anyone from the Advisory Committee, besides me, had visited the forest before the cut. But I already knew the answer to that. It was no.

When I think of that forest today, I think of the snails. None of us there that day, with our degrees and our state jobs, gave any thought to the snails. We had no idea what snail species were there, or in what abundance. The snails were never surveyed, or considered in the logging plans, or mentioned in my speech. But now that I have read the work of Daniel Douglas, I think of the snails.

Douglas examined the snail species in three forested areas of Kentucky. In each area he compared the snails found in an old-growth forest with those found in a nearby younger forest. At each site he collected from ten 1-hectare plots. Some snails were collected by hand, and others were collected by filling bags with leaf litter that was then dried, sieved, and examined by hand. In

Triodopsis tridentata, the disturbed-forest indicator snail.

total he collected more than three thousand snails. Using microscopes and keys, he identified seventy species of snail, all of them native. In every case the older forests contained more snail species. Overall, eighteen of the species were most common in old-growth forests. One of them in particular, *Carychium exile*, was the strongest indicator of an old-growth forest. I know that many things are compared to a grain of rice, but this little thing is literally the length (1.7 millimeters), color, and shape of a grain of white rice.

Another of the snail species, *Triodopsis tridentata*, was a strong indicator that a forest had been logged. This species, with a flat, reddish-brown shell and a dark-colored creature living inside, is almost the width of a dime—much larger than the tiny, white old-growth indicator.

Since they have both male and female reproductive structures, snails can self-reproduce, but normally they don't. In fact, snails are quite promiscuous and an average snail has mated with two to six different partners. Sperm is delivered in a packet called a spermatophore, which contains more than a million tiny sperm cells. It takes a snail three to four weeks to prepare and replenish a new spermatophore after one has been delivered. The female structures of a snail can store the multiple various spermatophores and control which ones will be used to fertilize its eggs.

Seventeen of the twenty indicator species for undisturbed old-growth forests were micro-snails, meaning they were less than 5 millimeters in size. Micro-snails are great indicators to use because they stay in one area for their whole lives, but this trait also makes them vulnerable to local extinction because they can neither escape from disturbance events taking place in the forest nor recolonize quickly after a disturbance. Douglas believes that some land snail species may become locally extinct from forests that are managed through intensive forestry, such as clear-cutting. And at the very least, disturbance of an old-growth forest leaves behind a different snail community, as his list of old-growth indicator snails shows.

The life histories and ecologies of many snails have never been studied; hence we must often generalize when we talk about snails. Snails can live for a number of years. They need an environmental source of calcium to build their shells. If no limestone is available in the environment, the snails may depend on deciduous trees that have leaves with a high calcium content, such as maple or dogwood. The snails themselves may then become an important source of calcium for small vertebrates such as shrews and salamanders. Snails may eat living plant material or litter on the forest floor. The presence of non-native worms in a forest may be detrimental because it reduces both these food sources. Snails also eat fungi and lichens, including the small calicioid lichens I discuss later in the book. This is not always detrimental to lichen populations, however, since the snails may also carry and disperse fragments of the lichens (in the same way that birds function as both predators and dispersers of plants).

Table 2. Snail species that are indicators for old-growth forests in central and eastern Kentucky

Carychium exile

Carychium nannodes

Cochilocopa moreseana

Collumella simplex

Gastrocopta armifera

Gastrocopta contracta

Gastrocopta pentodon

Gastrocopta procera

Gastrodonta interna

Glyphyalinia indentata

Glyphyalinia wheatleyi

Guppya sterkii

Haplotrema concavum

Hawaii miniscula

Mesomphix cupreus

Patera appressa

Punctum minutissimum

Striatura ferrea

Vallonia exentrica

Vertigo parvula

About one-quarter of southeastern US snail species are found in association with coarse woody debris (98 out of 401 species). Older forests generally contain higher levels of woody debris. Particular snail species are also found in association with woody debris from particular tree species. Therefore, simplifying a forest from a diverse native mixture to a forest managed for just one, or a few, marketable tree species has negative impacts on snail diversity. Forest management techniques, such as thinning, may also change microhabitats and create drought-like conditions that have negative impacts on forest snails. Douglas concludes, and it should come as no surprise, that "older and less disturbed forests are likely important for preserving biological diversity."

Here, then, is my stump speech for snails: "You snails who just lost your habitat, you snails baking in the sun, you snails who just got crushed beneath the logging machinery, I speak for you, too. I vow that in some places you shall be left in peace."

Sources on page 198.

7

Insects in the Forest

Have you ever been aware as you walked through a forest that everything you saw, heard, and even smelled was largely the result of insects? I wasn't, until Tim Schowalter enlightened me. I'm not talking just about pollinators here, as important as they are. Tim helped me see how the structure of old-growth forests before human intervention depended on the leaf-eating insects.

Just as we need large-animal predators to keep smaller prey species in check, we also need insects to keep plants in check. Instead of thinking of our native leaf-eating insects as injurious to plants, imagine them instead as tiny gardeners trimming here and there. These gardeners specialize in either the cone-bearing evergreen trees or the broad-leaved trees, but never both. Among those that specialize in the broad-leaved trees, some work on the whole group while others may work their whole lives on just one species in the group (like the yew trimmer in Kew Gardens). I'm having fun with the gardener concept here, but you know I'm talking about insects that feed only on particular kinds of leaves.

Trees, just like animal prey species, do not want to be someone's dinner, of course, but unlike voles, trees cannot run away. They are rooted in place and fight back primarily with the chemicals they produce. Their ability to do this has evolved over tens of millions of years. If not for being eaten, the trees would never have evolved to produce those chemical weapons. Tree leaves smell different from one another because of their specialized anti-insect chemistry. We have insects to thank for the pungent smell of a walnut leaf or the delight of breathing balsam-fir air on a cool, sunny day.

Ah, but the leaf-eating insects have another wild card—many of them have evolved the ability to detoxify those chemical weapons. Just as only a certain type of tree has the capacity to produce a certain type of chemical, only certain types of insects have the metabolic equipment to detoxify those chemicals. No tree can do it all, and no insect can do it all. The result of this arms race is that we have insects that feed only on cherry trees, insects that feed only on oak trees, insects that feed only on hemlocks, and so on.

When one tree species is highly successful, it is in danger of taking over the whole forest canopy. The insect species that feed specifically on that tree species then become more abundant too (because of the abundance of their "prey") and trim it back even more, thus keeping it in check and leaving space for other tree species. So the insects allow greater numbers of tree species to coexist. And greater diversity of tree species means greater diversity of leaf-eating insects (specialized gardeners) like tree crickets and katydids. And the forest sings with their songs. And the quieter leaf-eating insects, like the caterpillars, feed the birds that sing the song of the forest for them. The leaf-eating insects are a hugely important food source for migrating birds such as warblers. The birds are on the side of the trees in this game of thrones.

The leaf-eating insects have other foes as well, such as the predatory spiders and insects. Just like human hunters, spiders can either wait in ambush or go in search of a meal. It's a spider's smorgasbord up there in the canopy. And then there are the parasitoids. These flying insects do not kill the leaf eaters themselves; they pass that job along to their offspring. The parasitoids fly through the canopy sniffing for just the sort of leaf eater they specialize in; when they find one, they inject it with their eggs. The leaf eater continues climbing and munching while protecting and incubating the eggs of the parasitoid. Their reward for performing this service is being eaten from the inside out by the larvae when they hatch.

But it's really not as simple as all that (ha!); it's not just a game of win or lose. The leaf eaters may be helping the trees, too. As they chew the leaves, their feces, containing the masticated and digested leaves, are like sprinklings of compost. The sprinkles contain water-soluble nutrients that are then absorbed by the tree for making new leaves. Round and round.

June Jeffries and her team studied the plant-eating insects found on white oak trees in forests of various ages in Missouri, from newly harvested to old growth (more than 313 years old). Starting at ground level they searched the trunk, every twig, and both sides of at least 600 leaves on each sampled tree. They found more than 126 different species of insects, more than 8,200 individual leaf-eating insects in all. At certain times of year, insect species richness and density was higher in the older forests, but more important, a unique community of insects was found in the older forests. Four leaf-eating insects were significantly associated with only the older forests: the curve-lined looper, a twiggy-looking inchworm; the palmerworm, with one narrow and two wide stripes running down its back; the gold-striped leaftier, which makes silk and rolls itself into the leaf; and an oak leaf miner (*Phyllonorycter fitchella*) that is so uncommon I could find no images of it nor a common name.

Furthermore, the mix of insect species found in the forest continued to change, even when the forests hadn't been disturbed for more than two hundred years. Jeffries's team concluded that "adequate conservation of the insect fauna in forests of long-lived trees such as white oak may require longer time periods between timber harvests at the same location (extended rotation time) for some portion of the total forested landscape than is prescribed by current silvicultural practice." In other words, if we have only young forests, we will have only the insect communities found in young forests, and the insect communities that would have come later will come no more, resulting in a loss of biodiversity.

We all know that biodiversity is important. These small insects we are talking about here are the living things that have evolved before us and around us. They add to life's amazement. If we do nothing about what these scientists are telling us as they summarize their careful research, we are the ones responsible for the erosion of biodiversity on planet Earth. We have a choice. It's not that difficult. Save at least a little from the blade, from the plow, from the feller buncher.

But that is just a small part of the insect story in forests. Insects have every type of lifestyle imaginable. They inhabit niches from the very top of the canopy to beneath the forest floor. Of the 1.6 million described and named species of animals on earth, way more than half are insects. And of this multitude of insects, almost half are beetles. There is a story that when evolutionary biologist J. B. S. Haldane was asked what conclusion might be drawn about the nature of the Creator from a study of the creation, he answered, "An inordinate fondness for beetles." To put this comment in perspective, realize that about four hundred thousand beetle species have been identified (with many more likely yet to be discovered) and only nine thousand bird species. Bringing these numbers down to earth and a little closer to home, consider that Great Smoky Mountains National Park

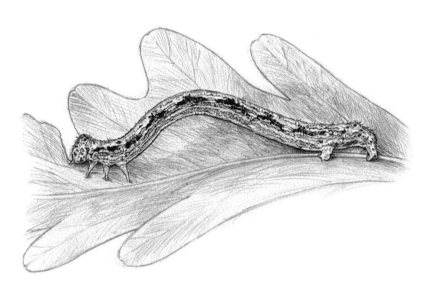

A curve-lined looper, found only in old-growth forests.

shelters 450 species of animals with backbones (this includes mammals, birds, amphibians, and the like), 2,816 species of plants, and more than 4,300 species of insects and spiders. How many of them can you identify?

Some insects, such as those discussed earlier, feed on living trees, while others require deadwood. More than half of all beetle species are in this second group; therefore, when we talk about beetles worldwide that depend on deadwood we are not talking about an insignificant group. We are talking about hundreds of thousands of species—more than all the birds, all the mammals, all the reptiles and amphibians combined. Way more.

And what is it that these poster creatures for biodiversity need in order to live healthy and successful lives? They need deadwood, and size does count: the bigger the better. A number of attributes of large deadwood make beetles want to call it home. Deadwood of large diameter generally contains many different types of habitat, allowing room for all the beetles to occupy their preferred niche.

Think of the difference between an efficiency apartment and a villa in France: if you were going to bring a dozen highly creative but very fussy artists together, where would you rather house them? (Scientists, you may make up your own ideal laboratory spaces here. . . .) The musicians need a music room (or two) where they can make noise, the writers need their own private quiet space, the artists need light and space to create without worrying about cleanliness, the cook needs space to prepare meals. And everyone needs a bathroom. You would choose the villa, of course. It is the same with the beetles—so many different species, all with different requirements. The deadwood in a young managed forest is like the efficiency apartment—fine for a few beetle species. But the deadwood in an old-growth forest is like the villa in France—with so many habitats to choose from there is something for even the fussiest beetles. (Instead of grand pianos and internet connections, fussy beetles look for just the right type of fungi rotting the wood, or just the right moisture levels.)

While I'm having fun with this comparison, let's extend it a little further. Both the fussy, artistic humans and the habitat-specific beetles depend on their shelter's permanence; it is part of what makes the place desirable. The artistic humans want to be able to return year after year, perhaps generation after generation, to the villa retreat, if it is around that long. They frequently choose a stable, familiar retreat over new ones that have been in existence for just a year or two. If the villa eventually needed to be demolished but they could occupy a great villa next door, they would easily shift their allegiance there. However, if the retreat space were moved to Kenya, the transition would be difficult, and many of the artists would never show up again. It is much the same with beetles—they need a space that will be there for years; small deadwood decomposes too quickly for them. The larger diameter deadwood that they prefer will decompose in time, of course, but beetles can shift to other deadwood if it exists nearby—which is likely in an old-growth forest. However, if the forest where they live is too heavily disturbed (perhaps by thinning or harvesting), some beetles are not successful at finding another older forest to occupy. They have a limited range of travel.

Most of the studies on beetles in old growth have been done in Scandinavia and Europe. Time and time again, rare beetles are found in the rare habitats of the older forests. Although studies have also been done in the United States linking the presence of large deadfall (also known as coarse woody debris) to beetle diversity and abundance, only one study has proposed using one of these beetles as an old-growth indicator. The proposed indicator is the round fungus beetle *Anistoma inops*, family Leiodidae.

I mentioned earlier just how many, many beetle species exist. In fact, because there are not enough common names to go around, many beetles are called round fungus beetle—3,500 species worldwide and 350 species in North America. These particular little creatures, about the size of a mini chocolate chip, feed on underground fungi and slime molds. The slime molds need a damp environment, and they often grow under the bark of rotting wood. Many more fungal species are found in old-growth forests than in younger forests, so it should be no surprise that this beetle is found there also. Its smooth domed shape allows it to easily squeeze into spaces in the rotting wood. Beetles like this have been found embedded in amber, so we know that they have been around for tens of millions of years, but they may or may not be around much longer—depending on how we choose to treat our forests.

A New Hampshire study conducted by Donald Chandler and Stewart Peck compared the number and species of round fungus beetles found in an old-growth forest called The Bowl with those found in a managed forest, Spring Brook, which had been selectively logged forty years before the study. Although the species differed, the total number of species in each forest was the same

Round fungus beetle—an old-growth indicator?

(thirty-four). The total number of individuals, however, was almost three times higher in the old growth, as shown in the table on pages 64–65.

Many insects feed on the conks (visible fruiting bodies) of shelf or bracket fungi that are instrumental in the decay of coarse woody debris. Because of this association, many of these insects, as well as the fungi on which they feed, are strongly associated with old-growth forests. One such species, the ironclad bark beetle (*Phellopsis obcordata*), is known primarily from old-growth balsam fir, hemlock, and birch forests in the Appalachian Mountains. These bumpy brown beetles play dead and drop to the ground when they are disturbed.

By managing forests so that standing wood is removed before it is allowed to decay, we eliminate large deadwood and at the same time a whole suite of beetle species that depend on large deadwood. We also reduce the food available for woodpeckers, and bears, and ground beetles that search deadwood for these beetles and their grubs. With successive timber-harvesting cycles, an increasing loss of beetle species is likely. These tales of deadwood-dependent beetles from here and abroad point out once again that if we want to keep all the pieces, we need to allow for natural dynamics in the landscape, including the occasional occurrence of pest and disease outbreaks, windthrow, and fire. We also need to allow either places that are not managed or management that offers the opportunity for at least some trees to live to maturity and decay without intervention.

We have discussed insects found on tree leaves and in deadwood, but many more habitats exist in the forest for insects. In almost any place you can imagine, an insect specializes in that habitat. For instance, some beetles are found only in the hollows of living trees. Young, intensively managed, "healthy" forests do not commonly have trees with hollows, so do not look for any of those beetles there.

In addition to deadwood- and fungal-feeding insects, insect predators are found on the forest floor as well. Erika Latty and her team studied the occurrence of a particular category of predaceous beetles—the ground beetles (family Carabidae)—in young, mature, and old-growth forests of northern Wisconsin and the Upper Peninsula of Michigan. They found that overall abundance and diversity of ground beetles didn't differ significantly between forest types, but, again, the old-growth forest

Table 3. Numbers of individual beetles of different species collected from the forest floor in two New Hampshire forests, old-growth The Bowl and forty-year-old Spring Brook

Species	The Bowl (old growth)	Spring Brook (managed)
Family Leiodinae		
Anisotoma basalis	54	8
Anisotoma blanchardi	0	1
Anisotoma errans	53	25
Anisotoma geminata	119	20
Anisotoma horni	798	133
Anisotoma inops	46	1
Agathidium assimile	15	4
Agathidium atronitens	17	9
Agathidium sp. near *concinnum*	9	13
Agathidium sp. near *depressum*	5	0
Agathidium sp. near *oniscoides*	70	32
Agathidium parvulum	93	56
Agathidium politum	73	15
Agathidium rusticum	77	35
Agathidium temporale	18	1
Leiodes assimilis	3	5
Leiodes conj	119	77
Leiodes impersonata	0	5
Leiodes mult	2	0
Leiodes soer	48	18
Leiodes vari	9	12
Colentis impunctata	28	31

Family Cholevinae

Catops americanus	305	196
Catops basilaris	1,029	303
Catops gratiosus	165	33
Catops simplex	228	127
Nemadus horni	17	2
Nemadus parasitus	0	3
Prionochaeta opaca	3	0
Sciodrepoides fumatus terminans	28	11
Sciodrepoides watsoni hornianus	36	8

Family Coloninae

Colon forceps	14	7
Colon hubbardi	7	0
Colon schwarzi	25	54
Colon sp. 4	2	0
Colon sp. 5	1	5
Colon rectum	1	6
Colon sp. 13	0	1
Colon horni	0	9
Total number of species	**34**	**34**
Total number of individuals	**3,517**	**1,266**

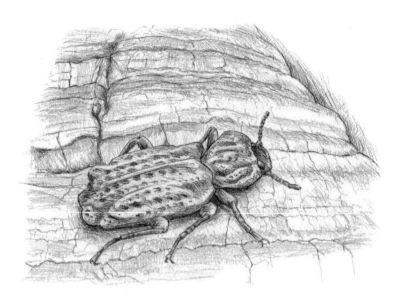

The ironclad bark beetle, which eats shelf fungus.

hosted a unique community. Five beetle species were considered indicators since as a group they had significant affiliations with the old-growth forests. Because so many beetles exist and so few people talk about them in the field, most species don't even have common names. You would not be corrected by an entomologist if you called each one of these a woodland ground beetle. Given that they look somewhat alike, try separating 47,590 of them into fifty-nine species! That is what these researchers did to determine how forest age influences ground beetles. I only wish they hadn't had to kill all those beetles to do it.

The northern hardwood–hemlock forest type they studied has changed massively in the past few hundred years, as shown in the table on page 68. This forest type now covers only a quarter of the land it did when European settlers arrived in northern Wisconsin and the Upper Peninsula, and only 0.4 percent of that is old-growth forest. These beetles don't have many places left to call home.

The predaceous woodland ground beetle, of which many
species exist (based on a photo by Scott Housten).

Table 4. Places a ground beetle can call home: Changes in the forest cover in northern Wisconsin and the Upper Peninsula of Michigan

Forest cover type	Proportion on pre-settlement landscape (%)	Proportion on current landscape (%)
Northern hardwood–hemlock	100	24
Unmanaged	100	0.5
Old-growth	63	0.4
Regenerating	37	0.1
Managed	0	23
≥Sixty years	0	16
Sixty years	0	7

What advice do these researchers give to ensure the preservation of these insect species? I'm sure it will come as no surprise to you: "Given forest reduction at the landscape scale and the nearly 100-percent loss of old-growth forest, we suggest that the conservation of carabid diversity is dependent on maintaining forests in a variety of age classes including late-successional stages."

We are fortunate in the United States that our forest destruction started so recently (just a few hundred years ago). The history of forest abuse in western Europe is altogether different. Simon Grove tells that story: "Forests had scarcely reached their maximum post-glacial extent when farmers started clearing them. Over the following millennia forest cover was drastically reduced, and the structure and composition of remaining fragments greatly altered. By 1000 A.D., there was probably no truly natural forest left in Europe outside Fennoscandia. It was not just wolves, bears, and lynx that retreated as forests were cleared." As the remaining fragments were intensively managed for firewood, poles, and other wood products, the old-growth forests disappeared and along with them many of the old-growth-dependent insects. The result is that many insect species have now vanished from those areas. In the United Kingdom, seventeen deadwood-associated insects are known only from peat deposits (2900 BC) and fossils. None of these species is yet globally extinct, but most now survive only in tiny refugia elsewhere in Europe.

Although forest cover is coming back in some areas of Europe, the beetle loss continues, largely due to intensive forest management that doesn't allow for large old trees to die and rot. The removal of mature timber habitat is considered the main threat for 65 percent of the United Kingdom's 150 threatened woodland insect species. Many of the old-growth-loving beetle species are hanging on in single small patches—or even single large old trees. It's not difficult to imagine how just one unfortunate event could cause further local—and possibly global—extinctions.

Then there are the tiniest creatures on the forest floor, so tiny they can make a meal of bacteria. I am thinking of the mites. There are forty-eight thousand different kinds of mite (try telling *them* apart!), with every lifestyle imaginable, but the ones most likely to be found on the forest floor are the oribatid mites—and there are only six thousand different kinds of them. (Chiggers are mites, but not oribatids.) In a study of mites in differently aged forests in South Carolina and North Carolina, some species were found in the old-growth forests that did not occur in the younger forests, but overall the density of the mites was higher in the younger forest. I wish someone would do this research regarding the chigger mite (family Trombiculidae). If fewer chiggers were found per inch in the ancient forests, we might have many more people interested in preserving them.

Speaking of "problem insects," Latty's study of those many, many beetles found five non-native beetle species—all of them associated with the managed forests but not the old-growth forests. Are the managed forests really the healthiest? Not if you are a native insect or a tree.

So let's ask and answer our recurring questions: In terms of insects, are there any differences between young forests and old-growth forests? Absolutely! Many insects depend on the presence of ancient forests and will become extinct without them. Are there any indicator species that are more likely to be found in old growth? Yes! But good luck trying to tell them apart; this is a job for the experts.

Sources on pages 198–99.

8

Herbaceous Plants in the Forest

Okay, so you lost that battle. The forest came down or is about to come down. The foresters assure you that the species in the forest will return. You try to reassure yourself by telling yourself the same thing: *It will heal in time. I may not live to see it, but it will heal.*

But will it really? What do we know about that? With all the times that this assurance has been offered, it is surprising how infrequently it has been tested. And there are many ways to assess healing: we can monitor the trees, or the lichens, or the animals (such as snails). Another way to monitor the return of biodiversity is through the small plants that grow on the forest floor. These small plants, generally shorter than chin height, are described using different names; sometimes they are called the ground vegetation, sometimes the herbaceous layer, and sometimes just herbs for short. The herbs in a forest are not always edible like the ones in your kitchen cabinet—they include ferns and spring wildflowers and other plants you might label as weeds. For the purposes of our discussion, we will not include tiny tree seedlings.

Although these ground-layer plants make up only 1 percent of the plant biomass of a forest, they account for 90 percent of the plant diversity. Many more species live on the ground than in the canopy, and the diversity of all other organisms in a forest, from butterflies to mammals, is more closely correlated with herbaceous plant diversity than it is with tree species diversity.

Beyond their edibility and beauty, these plants don't always appear useful to us humans, but every plant in the forest has one or more different partners. Some partners are helpful and others are harmful (when labeled narrowly); the pollinators, the herbivores, the dispersers, and the fungi all interact in a way unique to a particular plant species. So biodiversity on the herb level means biodiversity spread out to many other levels as well. No one has had the time or tools to study it *all*, but those who have studied the herbaceous plants have something to tell us: once you clear-cut an old-growth forest, the herbaceous layer *never* fully recovers. It is possible that cutting may result in more diversity in the short-term (because annual sun-loving plants are quick to germinate), but the perennial spring wildflowers that grow in shady forests and depend on ants for seed distribution are permanently impaired by clear-cut logging.

In 1980 Richard Brewer published a study done in a beech and sugar-maple forest in Michigan that had been undisturbed for 150 years. He used surveys of the herbaceous vegetation done in 1920, again in 1933, and again in 1974. He found that the plant populations had changed, but that they really weren't increasing or decreasing in species richness. This indicated to him that the forest didn't seem to be recovering from the disturbance 150 years earlier. Brewer concluded that the forest was depauperate in many species when compared to true old-growth forests and that it would likely remain so.

A few years after Brewer's paper, a study done in Lincolnshire, England, compared the herbaceous plants found in ancient woodlands (originating before 1600) with those occurring in recent woodlands (those originating between 1600 and 1820). Note that many of these "recent" woods are old enough to be considered old growth by many of today's researchers. They found that the ancient woods were richer in species than the recent woods. Once a forest is cleared, the researchers concluded, the soil is altered in such a way that many species either cannot return or have not returned in hundreds of years. In their words: "Claims that secondary woods will one day become as rich as ancient, presumed primary, woods seem unfounded."

It was not until the 1990s that studies began addressing the recovery of herbaceous diversity in eastern US forests. In 1992 David Duffy and Albert Meier compared nine old-growth forests in Georgia, Kentucky, North Carolina, and Tennessee with second-growth forests occurring near each. The secondary forests varied in age from forty-five to eighty-seven years. They found that in all cases the old-growth forests had greater species richness and greater plant cover.

In a follow-up paper they examined how the forest floor gets damaged during clear-cutting and why the herbaceous layer doesn't recover. First, there is the direct damage to the plants on the forest floor caused by the logging equipment. Second, when a forest is clear-cut and the tree canopy is removed, the nutrients vital to the functioning of that forest are removed along with the trees. In a natural situation, when these trees died they would have returned their nutrients to the forest floor where the herbaceous plants (with the help of fungi) could benefit. Third, the increased temperatures and increased sunlight on the ground caused by logging are damaging to shade-adapted plants. This change in microclimate often results in drought conditions and death for small plants that may have survived being destroyed in the logging operations. Conversely, some herbaceous plants do well with extra sunlight and require the gaps in a canopy that occur when a mature tree falls. But after a clear-cut, the forest that returns is even aged and gaps may be rare for the first eighty years. These deep-forest, yet light-dependent, plants may not be able to survive in the shade of an even-aged forest for the decades it takes for gaps to begin occurring regularly.

Once these native plant populations have been disrupted, they are prevented from successful reestablishment by another set of factors. One factor is invasive species that may be introduced or encouraged as a result of the clearing. These invasive species might be plants, such as the polygonums (like mile-a-minute weed and Japanese knotweed), or they might be animals, such as non-native worms. Second, woodland native plant species are often dispersed by ants, and in the absence of a nearby ancient forest it could be many, many years (perhaps hundreds) before an extirpated species is naturally reintroduced. And once the seeds have reached the forest and found conditions suitable for germination (sometimes requiring a fungal partnership), it may take up to a decade for the plant to reach sexual maturity and start producing its own seeds. In addition, once a plant has successfully established itself, the average vegetative spread is surprisingly slow—less than 2 centimeters per year. This is less than the width of your fingernail! No wonder herbaceous plants recolonize so slowly that the tree species recover before they do. Is complete recovery of herbaceous forest plant populations even possible? If so, it requires more than several centuries and we haven't seen it happen yet.

At the risk of sending you into a fatal depression, I haven't even mentioned the complicating factors of climate change, acidification, ozone depletion, and nitrogen deposition. All of these have been shown to influence herbaceous vegetation in some way. In conclusion, Meier and his team note that "the low to non-existent recovery rates observed for vernal forest herbs suggest that even a landscape of hypothetically restored, old, secondary

Hobblebush (*Viburnum alnifolium*), a woody plant species often found in old growth (based on a photo by Nicholas A. Tonelli / Flickr, CC BY 2.0).

forest may not serve to conserve and restore vernal-herb populations. Management plans should therefore include protection of remaining primary, mixed, mesophytic forests."

In a 2009 study, Anthony D'Amato and colleagues examined old-growth (300-plus-year-old) and second-growth (100-to-175-year-old) hemlock forests in western Massachusetts. In addition to the herbaceous plants, they also recorded the presence and abundance of shrubs and small trees. Of the forty-seven plant species identified, twenty-nine occurred only in the old-growth sites. Like previous researchers, they found that the old-growth forest study areas had greater ground-level species diversity, richness, and plant cover. They attributed this difference to the greater abundance of natural tree-fall gaps in the older forests, and the increase in coarse woody debris. They

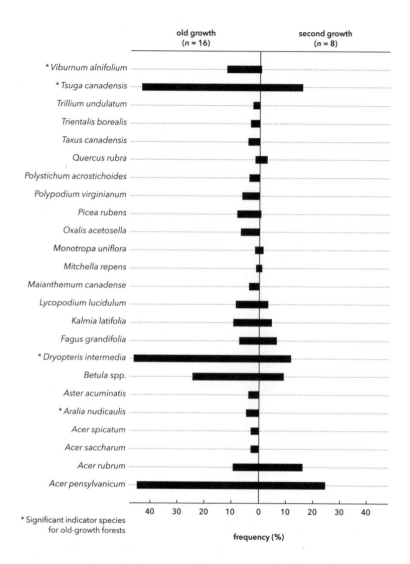

* Viburnum alnifolium
* Tsuga canadensis
Trillium undulatum
Trientalis borealis
Taxus canadensis
Quercus rubra
Polystichum acrostichoides
Polypodium virginianum
Picea rubens
Oxalis acetosella
Monotropa uniflora
Mitchella repens
Maianthemum canadense
Lycopodium lucidulum
Kalmia latifolia
Fagus grandifolia
* Dryopteris intermedia
Betula spp.
Aster acuminatis
* Aralia nudicaulis
Acer spicatum
Acer saccharum
Acer rubrum
Acer pensylvanicum

40   30   20   10   0   10   20   30   40

* Significant indicator species
for old-growth forests

frequency (%)

Average frequency of occurrence of common plant species within sixteen old-growth and eight second-growth eastern hemlock forests in western Massachusetts (Anna Eshelman, based on original by D'Amato, Orwig, and Foster). Asterisks indicate significant indicator species for old-growth forests.

Wild sarsaparilla (*Auralia nudicaulis*), another plant often found in old growth.

found two woody plant species and one herbaceous plant species that were indicators for old-growth forests. The woody species were hobblebush (*Viburnum alnifolium*) and wild sarsaparilla (*Aralia nudicaulis*)—species that had also been identified by previous researchers as more common in old-growth forests. The herbaceous species was the intermediate woodfern (*Dryopteris intermedia*). These old-growth indicator species are fairly common. All occur over much of the eastern United States and Canada, and I have seen them myself on many disturbed sites, yet for some reason they did not occur in the second-growth stands in this study—most likely because of the unbroken shade there.

There is more to share about herbaceous plants in the forest. Julie Wyatt and Miles Silman followed up on Meier's work, adding much fancier statistical analyses but comparing just three old-growth and three mature forests in the Southeast instead of the nine that Meier had studied. Their results confirm what he found: "Current forestry management is not conducive to long-term maintenance of herb diversity."

If you feel moved to wander your favorite woodland and look for some of the herbaceous plants they found associated with old growth, here are three to get you started: spotted geranium (*Geranium maculatum*), northern maidenhair fern (*Adiantum pedatum*), and sweet white violet (*Viola blanda*). Notably, maidenhair fern and another round-leaf violet were found only in the old-growth forests in the D'Amato study, too. Again, these are not at all rare species, but there is something about forest disturbance and regrowth that they, or their symbiotic partners, do not like.

Since so little true old-growth forest is left and we are starting to recognize its importance, a type of specialized forest management has recently been developed for the purpose of creating or hastening old-growth attributes in older second-growth forests. Picture a person with a chain saw felling a tree, or a few, to create a gap in the canopy of the type that would exist in old growth. The tree is left lying on the forest floor to decompose, thus adding large coarse woody debris to the ecosystem. Other trees are girdled to create standing deadwood (snags) or hacked at to create cavities for wildlife. A shovel might be used to create pit-and-mound topography. All these things would happen on their own, of course—given another hundred years or so. In its purest form this sort of management would likely increase the diversity and cover of herbaceous plants on the forest floor, and it could increase animal habitat as well. But it could also increase the likelihood of invasive plants and worms (through seeds and eggs carried on workers' boots), which would then decrease the numbers of native herbaceous plants. There is no right answer here, but some tend toward less management and some tend toward

Northern maidenhair fern (*Adiantum pedatum*), a ground-level plant more common in old-growth forests (based on a photo by Tom Lockhart).

more. I am one of those who tend toward less, as I have seen what more can do.

When we walk through the oldest forest near our town—most likely an eighty-something-year-old forest—we may be enthralled by the woodland vegetation and the towering trees without ever realizing what we are missing. We see clear-cut forests that seem to be recovering in our lifetimes, and we may start believing that all is well. And some research shows this, too. But a closer look at that particular research shows that often the forest used for baseline comparison is only 100 to 150 years old. So little old-growth forest remains in the eastern United States that researchers don't even have good study plots to choose from. One result is that our baselines are shifting. We don't even know what forests should look like anymore. Do we notice that the forest we are walking through has fewer herbaceous plants and fewer types of herbaceous plants than it had once upon a time? No, because we have likely never experienced a forest like that near our town. We don't even know what's possible. Writer and biologist Robert Michael Pyle calls this "the extinction of experience." How can we miss what we don't know? Organisms have their own specific needs of the landscape, Pyle notes, and when these cease to be met they vanish.

And the same can be said of people, I guess. Writing about this topic and rereading Pyle's essay in *The Thunder Tree* have gotten me a bit down. From 2012 to 2016 I worked to save a beautiful little forest in the heart of Salisbury, Maryland. It was one of the rare local forests that had never been completely clear-cut. It contained the largest, and I'd wager the oldest, pond pine in the state of Maryland. The forest had impressively large oaks, beeches, maples, sycamores, and tulip poplars. It had Atlantic white cedar trees—the same tree species that has gone extinct in the adjacent state of Pennsylvania, and the same species the State of Maryland and The Nature Conservancy have spent tens (hundreds?) of thousands of dollars to restore. No one ever surveyed the forest floor; it was destroyed before we had a chance to.

Aldo Leopold says that to get an ecological education is to live in a world of wounds. Carl Safina puts it another way: "The more I sense the miracle, the more intense appears the tragedy." Pyle says that natural green spaces are the bandages and the balm for those wounds. He says, "We all need spots near home where we can wander off a trail, lift a stone, poke about, and merely wonder." I wanted this sweet forest to be one of those places. But it was in the "metro core" and the developer who owned it, Brad Gillis, planned to cut the forest and put in ninety townhomes.

I talked to him about it, and told him what a special place it was. I pleaded with the mayor, I talked with the local land trust, I described the forest and the threats to it in the local paper, I took university teachers and students there. I called the state's Department of Natural Resources, I wrote up a position paper, I called the Trust for Public Land, and other groups, but no one offered any useful assistance. Like a forest herb without the right conditions and the right partners, I failed. In 2016 Gillis sent in the trucks and the chainsaws, and the forest came down. According to the city planning department he had the right to do so, but I will never believe that it was right to do so. Five years have passed since then, the money gotten from the timber is likely earning interest, but nothing has been built. There is only a scar there.

I think about that forest often. What could I have done better? I realize now, too late, that the only thing that developer was interested in was money. He would have sold the forest for a large enough profit. At the time I had no fundraising experience on that large a scale, and I had no partners willing to help, so perhaps I could be forgiven. But I do not forgive myself. I still feel that I failed generations of children in our town, as well as all the organisms that used to live in that forest. But out of that pain and regret has grown a strength. I do not back down so easily now, and the organization I founded, the Old-Growth Forest Network, helps others that are facing similar situations in their towns.

Developers stimulating the economy did not save those rare old-growth forests where we have just started to learn the story of the forest herbs; they were saved by individuals who wanted to keep experience alive, who found true value in biodiversity, value beyond a bank balance. They didn't have the research we do today on the forest plants; they just *knew*. They knew already what Julie Wyatt and Miles Silman have since written and published: "Multiple forest stands in the landscape need to be removed from the logging rotation along with the preservation of all remnant old-growth forests."

Sources on pages 199–200.

9

Mosses in the Forest

In 2001, concerned about the conversion of mature native forests to pine plantations in my community, I decided to initiate an ecological study to show how this could negatively affect biodiversity and why, therefore, we should stop the cutting and conversion. I cast about for a good study organism to use (snails? spiders?) and thought that perhaps bryophytes (mosses and liverworts) would be just the thing. They were in the plant kingdom (my area of expertise), they held still, and they didn't bite. Although I had been identifying plants for decades by then, I didn't have any experience identifying mosses beyond the few most common ones. How hard could it be? Well, I found out promptly when I invited a local expert on a field trip. My head was spinning! Maybe it would have to be snails after all.

I tell this funny little story because it points out not only my own personal hubris (always healthy to get out of the closet) but it also reminds us of how dedicated one must be to learn the collection methods, features, and vocabulary of a specialized field. And beyond that, one must actually get out in the field, or back in the lab, often enough that the knowledge doesn't fade. Not to mention keeping up with the other studies . . . and the name changes. Studying each of the life forms we have been talking about (mosses, lichens, fungi, insects, herbaceous plants, amphibians, snails) is so time consuming on its own that you will never meet anyone who is expert in all of them.

So what happened to my incipient study? I gave it some thought and determined that whatever organisms I used, it would take me at least six months to become familiar with the organisms and the background studies, and to design a proper study. It would probably take another year or two to complete the study, then another six months to write a paper and get it published. If I did a fabulous job at all of this, perhaps I would be published in a very important journal such as *Ecology* or *Science* or *Nature*.

And then what? Would that do anything to slow the clear-cutting of forests in my community? Doubtful.

When I took a look at the scientific papers (the literature, as academics call it) that showed the erosion of biodiversity resulting from clear-cutting, I decided that those scientists were already doing a great job. Something that could perhaps make more of a difference than adding to this pile of research would be writing about the studies that had already been done. In 2005 that idea turned into the book *Teaching the Trees*. So I became an author, but I never did become an expert on mosses. My brief brush with bryophyte research did, however, give me a deep appreciation for those who are experts, such as Gregory McGee and Robin Wall Kimmerer.

You might appreciate their expertise even more when you realize that the majority of humans do not know the difference between a lichen and a moss. In fact, a highly intelligent, degreed, well-read person just asked me about that last night. So I told her that the two types of organisms have some things in common: they can both grow on tree trunks (and other surfaces), they both make their energy through photosynthesis, and they are very roughly the same size. Other than that, however, they are completely different. We may as well be comparing a mushroom and a millipede.

It is always a delicate matter to suggest groupings of biological organisms since so many fuzzy areas exist between groups. The result is that the groups and the group names change frequently—depending on the latest research and the loudest voices. Just as I watched atmospheric carbon dioxide levels change during my two decades of teaching, so did I watch almost every new edition of textbooks use a different grouping system. So just for this discussion, although it is likely not the final word, if we say that all living things are grouped into six categories (called kingdoms at the moment), then mosses and liverworts are in the kingdom Plantae. But lichens are not plants at all; they contain members of the kingdom Protista and the kingdom Fungi (and sometimes also bacterial partners from the other two kingdoms). The only kingdom left out, then, when we consider mosses and lichens is the kingdom Animalia.

Let's turn here to the bryophytes, the division of the kingdom Plantae that contains mosses and liverworts. They are true plants, as I mentioned, but ones that came along very early in plant evolution. They evolved from a type of algae that floated in shallow freshwater seas and managed to take hold at the land margin and survive on the waterlogged floodplains. This algal species could reproduce both asexually and sexually. For sexual reproduction, sperm were released into the water and made their way to the female reproductive structures. Over tens of millions of years (approximately 510 to 450 million years ago), the algal species evolved to survive greater and greater periods of desiccation. One way it did that was by harboring its fertilized embryos within and eventually releasing spores that were somewhat tolerant of drying. Slowly the plant form we call moss evolved. The mosses still produce swimming sperm, but the sperm either have to travel through a surface film of water (such as dew) or be carried by tiny soil insects (such as mites). Evidence exists that some soil insects are attracted to the moss reproductive structures in the same way that pollinators are attracted to flowers (so the kingdom Animalia is involved after all).

Mosses and liverworts share this common history and are closely related, but in mosses the leaf-like scales can stick out in any direction and the spore-bearing capsules often stick up into the air, while the liverworts appear flatter since their leafy scales emerge in no more than three planes. The classification lines separating them are thin.

It is always interesting to me, and somewhat of a mystery, that some of the bacteria species that evolved into algae are still present on earth. And the algae species that evolved into mosses are still present on earth. And some of the moss species that evolved into trees are still present on earth—just as the apes we share a common ancestor with are still present on earth. Not everything gets moved to the front of the line. Sometimes a step disappears—such as the early mammals that returned to the ocean—but sometimes they remain with us. As always, some must change to survive, and others must stay as they are to survive. And without those earlier evolved forms that are still here, this planet would be a much less functional, less interesting, less beautiful place.

So hooray to the mosses and liverworts that have stuck around for hundreds of millions of years and have found a reliable partner in the massive trees that are related to them but have been here a much shorter time. Without the forests of the world, we would lose many bryophyte species. Unfortunately, we have probably already lost some species with the worldwide decline in ancient forests.

What do we know about that, our central question? Do

Anomodon rugelii, a moss found in old-growth forests (based on a photo by Jim Stasz).

bryophyte species differ between older and younger forests? Could any bryophyte species be indicators of old-growth forests? That brings us back to our experts, McGee and Kimmerer, who did the work to try to answer those questions.

Upper New York State's Adirondack Park contains the largest acreage of uncut forest in the northeastern United States, and many eastern old-growth forest researchers carry out their studies in the park. McGee and Kimmerer chose forests there with three different histories: old growth (more than 175 years old); maturing (recovering from intense fire 90 to 100 years earlier); and intensively managed (no ages given). For each forest category they collected mosses from four different stands. In each stand they sampled the bryophytes and recorded the species of the tree, diameter of the tree, and height above ground level. Altogether they identified twenty-eight different bryophyte species.

Some of the species, like *Ulota crispa* and *Hypnum pallescens*

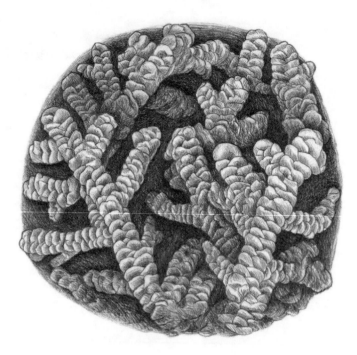

Porella platyphylloidea, a liverwort found in old-growth forests.

(low-growing types that can survive in a drier environment), were more abundant in the recently cut forests; other species (the more erect types) were more abundant in the old growth. These old-growth-loving bryophytes—*Anomodon rugelii* (a moss), *Neckera pennata* (a moss), and *Porella platyphylloidea* (a liverwort)—were all found growing on sugar maples, white ash, and American linden. These three tree species have thick, corky bark with higher moisture-holding capacity. And the older and larger these trees become, the thicker their bark gets and the longer it can hold moisture. The larger the diameter of the tree, the more likely these researchers were to find these three bryophyte species growing on it. It is probably this unique microhabitat, created by these particular trees above a certain age, that supplies the needs of these unique organisms.

Neckera pennata, another moss found in old-growth forests.

So yes, bryophyte species differ between older and younger forests. And bryophyte species exist that could be indicators of old-growth forests. I think I could learn to identify these three species for starters, and I know what trees to look for them on. Can't wait for my next journey into the old-growth forests of Adirondack Park.

Sources on page 200.

10

Fungi in the Forest

When I was a young girl attending summer camp, I participated in scavenger hunts. Each small team of children was given a list of items to find, and the first group to collect all of the items was awarded a prize. If you were given such a list today and "mushroom" was on the list, where would you look? Assuming purchased mushrooms would not count, you would probably head to the forest.

We often assume that the trees are creating the right habitat for the fungi, but it would be just as correct to assume that the fungi are creating the right habitat for the trees. Without fungi our forests would not look at all as they do now. One of the allures of the forest ecosystem is that it seems to provide for itself with no outside care. No one needs to prune or water or fertilize the forest trees. Ah, but here's a catch: the trees certainly rain down upon their roots all sorts of nutrient-rich particles, from pollen to blossoms to leaves to twigs, but the trees cannot feast on this food directly. They depend on an intermediary to digest the food first, and in the forest that predigester is most frequently a fungus.

A word here about vocabulary. You might have noticed that I already switched from talking about mushrooms to talking about fungi, but the two are not exactly the same. All mushrooms are fungi, but not all fungi are mushrooms. Fungi is a broad and very large group of organisms that are not plants, not animals, not bacteria, and not other types of one-celled organisms. To some they are kind of a leftover group, and strangely they are genetically more closely related to animals than to plants. But beyond what they are *not* is the fascinating range of what they *are*. Some fungi are microscopic and live only inside plant cells; some are microscopic and live only on the outside of animal cells. Some live only on living organisms, some live only on dead organisms, and some live only on scat. Some can live in salty environments and still others can live in environments that are scorching hot. One fungus even lassos tiny wormlike soil organisms and then feeds on their bodies.

As you might imagine, with so many different lifestyles, fungi also have many different life cycles. Only some fungi form the large spore-bearing structures we call mushrooms. These are the most fun to study, of course, because one can wander through the forest and say, "There's one!" and "There's another!" and sometimes take them home for dinner if they are the right kind. Also, if you are one who studies these mushrooms, as you walk across the forest floor you have the awareness that you are walking over a spongy mattress made of living threads. You don't walk on soil, like others do; you walk on a bed of mycelia—filaments tunneling through the soil from hundreds, perhaps thousands, of different fungus species. Even if there is not a mushroom in sight, you know the mycelia are there.

A mushroom is nothing like a plant, where you tuck a seed in the ground and give water, sunshine, and time, and voilà— you have a full-sized plant. To grow a mushroom you start with a microscopic spore. The spore germinates and grows into a microscopic filament (a hypha); that grows until at last it finds another filament of its same species and merges. This is fungal sex, but we call the strands plus and minus instead of male and female. The strands, now thicker and longer, grow (perhaps for years and perhaps covering many acres) until the entire spongy underground mass is triggered—generally by temperature and moisture changes—to form a mushroom. It is this huge underground support system that enables mushrooms to spring up literally overnight. Among those who study such things, the mushrooms are called the fruiting bodies of the fungi. Just as the fruits from a tree are the culmination of a long process with the biological purpose of spreading the genes in its seeds far and wide, the mushrooms are also designed to spread genes throughout the environment. These genes are packaged inside spores that are literally everywhere. Chances are that you are breathing fungus spores this very moment.

For something so ubiquitous in our environment, you would think that we would know more about them; the fact, however, is that we have no idea even of how many species exist. Approximately 100 thousand species have been identified and named, but the estimates are that there could be up to 5 million species. A decade ago the estimate was 1 million species, but newer scientific techniques that can identify species by examining DNA in the environment—instead of collecting and examining organisms (the former method of identification)—have led to a new awareness of fungal diversity. For example, Lee Taylor's research group at the University of Alaska Fairbanks used molecular methods to study the fungi they collected from the forest soil. In a 0.25-gram sample (about the amount of dirt a fingernail can hold), they found 218 species of fungus. When they took another sample in the same forest just three feet away, they found just as many species, but the big surprise was that fewer than 15 percent were species they had found in the first sample. Furthermore, the most common species in the first sample did not turn out to be the most common species in the second sample. Results like this led Taylor to an upward revising of estimates of fungal diversity.

These researchers found, among other things, that the most common fungi did not vary from year to year but did vary from season to season. Most of the species had some sort of association with plants. Some species were found primarily in the top, organic layer of soil, while others were generally found lower down in the mineral layer; still others were common in all layers. It is also likely that various fungi specialize in decomposing certain types of compounds.

If you are interested in a science with lots of room to grow and fascinating new discoveries, soil fungi studies may be just the thing for you.

The more we look at what is happening between trees and fungi, the more interesting things get. You already know that trees depend on fungi to decompose dead plant and animal parts, and to deliver nutrients in the basic chemical forms that trees can absorb; but fungi also extend the reach of trees far beyond the scope of their roots. The fungi, entwined intricately with the roots, can grow out beyond them and bring water and nutrients back to the tree from distant parts of the forest. In return, these mycorrhizae ("fungus roots") get something they cannot produce themselves: carbon compounds like sugar. Trees produce the carbon-containing sugars through the process of photosynthesis. High up in the canopy where the sun shines on tree leaves, the leaf cells draw in carbon dioxide and manufacture sugars from this raw material. A significant proportion of the sugars are then transported down to the tree roots. In the intimate space between the thinnest tree roots and the frail fungal mycelia, nutrients, water, and sugars are traded. Without this transfer both tree and fungus might die. It is estimated that 20 percent of the sugar produced by a tree enters the soil fungus network, and sometimes that figure is much higher.

We used to think that the organic carbon in forest soil was a result of leaves and twigs falling to the ground. But new research has shown that in old-growth boreal forests, the majority of the carbon in the soil is coming from below ground—from the roots and the fungal mycelia associated with them. The carbon is removed from the atmosphere and transported to the soil, where it is stored. And the older the forest is, the deeper this carbon-containing soil zone goes.

Researchers at the University of British Columbia found that Douglas fir trees in an upland forest were interconnected by mycelia, with the largest, oldest trees serving as hubs, much like the hub of a spoked wheel. Suzanne Simard calls these the "Mother Trees." One tree had connections to forty-seven other trees through this fungal network. New seedlings had the best chance of surviving when they connected to a common mycelium shared with big old trees. The extra nutrients and water provided by the fungi make trees more disease and drought resistant. Single strains of some fungal mycelia have been shown to cover hundreds of acres and connect thousands of trees.

Some of the mycorrhizal fungi are species specific—connecting trees of a common species together underground. Other fungal species are more inclusive, networking different species of trees throughout the forest. Again, some of the most interesting research on this topic was done in British Columbia. Researchers there found that Douglas fir and paper birch trees were linked by mycelia networks that allowed them to share resources. In the early spring when the birches weren't yet photosynthesizing, the evergreen Douglas firs could share sugars with them through their fungal connections. Later in the summer the leafy birches shared some of their resources with the shaded Douglas fir seedlings, and the shade they cast on the soil had a positive effect on the transfer. Then in the fall when the birches lost their leaves, the Douglas firs again shared their resources with the birches. These transfers were discovered by following labeled carbon molecules, bringing an entirely new understanding of how trees of different species can affect each other positively.

Imagine, then, what happens when a logger comes through to remove even just a few specially selected trees from a forest. The roots connected to the stump die, and eventually the fungal strands intertwined with those specific roots die also. The whole community of trees feels the loss through the change in the fungal network connecting them. Keeping the largest "hub trees" could make the forest as a whole healthier and more resilient. And beneath the trees are other, smaller plants (like orchids) that depend on soil fungi for germination. These plant species, and the animals that feed on them and the pollinators that visit them, also have a stake in the health of the fungal network.

New research is allowing us to understand much more about how plants communicate with one another and how fungi are involved in that process. Since plants are rooted in place with no ability to run away or call for help, they must defend themselves solely with the chemicals they produce or the other species they can attract and enlist in their aid. Many of the plant-produced chemicals evaporate easily into the atmosphere (hence their scientific name: volatile organic compounds). Insects can use these chemical scents to find the specific plants they want to eat or lay their eggs on. If you have ever wondered how tomato hornworm caterpillars always seem to find your tomato plants no matter where you put them, it is thanks to chemicals given off by the tomato leaves. The chemicals signal hawk moths that this is where they should lay the eggs that hatch into the voracious green monsters that can strip your precious tomato plant of all its leaves.

Tiny aphids also use these plant scents to find the plants they want to suck sap from. But the plants do not simply stand idle while the life is sucked from them; in response to an aphid invasion the composition of scents given off by plants changes and becomes repellent to other aphids flying by. These new scents can even attract the insects that parasitize aphids! So the plant has now elicited help in ridding itself of the aphids, without moving at all.

If this were not amazing enough, plants can also use these evaporative chemicals to communicate with other plants and warn them of threats. Acacia trees produce tannin to defend their leaves when animals graze upon them. The airborne scent of the tannin is picked up by other acacia trees, which then start to produce higher levels of tannin themselves as a protection from the nearby animals.

More recently, researchers have discovered that not only are these communicative chemical scents given off from the leaves and able to move through the atmosphere, but they are also exuded by the roots and move through the pores in the soil. Therefore, fungal filaments can carry chemical messages not only from plant to plant but throughout the forest.

At first glance the science experiment that demonstrates that this is possible seems deceptively simple. Take eight plastic drinking cups and fill them with soil that has been inoculated with mycorrhizal fungi. These are your replicates. Into each cup, plant five seedlings. Each of the seedlings will have a different treatment. Individually cover all five tiny plants in each cup with a clear film that can contain and channel airborne scents, and contain or exclude aphids. Contain the belowground parts of some of the seedlings, too: to one from each group, add mesh small enough to exclude both fungi and other roots; to a second, add mesh that excludes roots but not fungi. For a third seedling that has roots and fungi connected originally, break the connections;

allow the fourth plant to connect freely underground with the central, aphid-exposed, seedling.

The air samples collected from the central aphid-infested plant are able to repel aphids and attract aphid parasites, as expected, but the most interesting result is that the air samples from the plants connected to the aphid-infested plant only by underground fungi also repel the aphids and attract the parasites (the opposite of the entirely unconnected plant). The conclusion, then, is that plants can communicate through underground fungal connections.

These experiments have not been done on trees growing in forests yet. As you can imagine, that would be quite a bit more difficult than dealing with disposable cups in a laboratory, but it seems reasonable to me that the lab results could be extrapolated to forests. One might wonder how acting as a messenger would benefit the fungi, but realizing that aphids extract and utilize vast amounts of sugars from the trees—the same sugars the mycorrhizae depend on—one can see how the signaling may be in the best interests of the fungi.

Let us return now to our central questions: Will an older forest have more fungus species? Do some fungi grow only in older forests? And by extension: Can any fungi indicate to us that we are in an ancient forest?

Since fungi are so numerous, so varied in habitats, and often so small, we concern ourselves here with just the macrofungi, what we have been calling mushrooms—in other words, fungal fruiting bodies that can be seen aboveground with the naked eye.

European studies of mushrooms found in variously aged forests are well ahead of those in the eastern United States. Researchers there found not only more mushroom species in older forests, but more than four times more rare mushroom species in the old forests compared to the younger, managed forests. The higher numbers of rare fungi species were correlated with

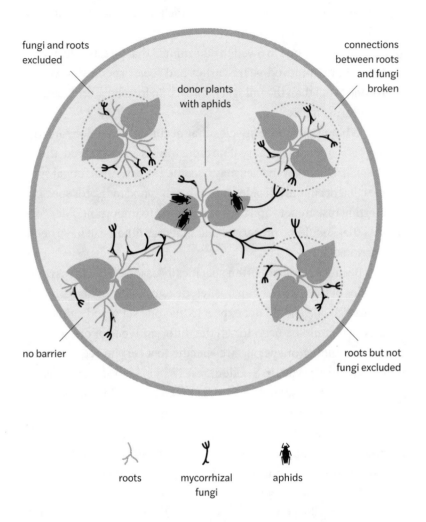

fungi and roots
excluded

connections
between roots
and fungi
broken

donor plants
with aphids

no barrier

roots but not
fungi excluded

roots

mycorrhizal
fungi

aphids

An experiment with bean seedlings growing in the same container to show
that plants can communicate through fungal contact alone (Anna Eshelman,
adapted from Babikova et al.).

higher numbers of rare plant and animal species. The only way to preserve these rare fungi is to preserve the rare and endangered habitats that contain them.

Research done in Sweden determined that forests selectively logged one hundred years earlier had fewer species of wood-rotting fungi than the unlogged forests. So forest disturbance has long-term effects.

What about these species that occur only in older forests? This is significant because if no older forests are preserved, those specialized fungal species may become extinct. Also, fungal species that occur only in older forests can be good indicator species, alerting researchers and conservationists to important older forests that should be preserved and that may otherwise have been overlooked.

Because fungi are often specifically associated with certain species of trees (either as parasites, decomposers, or mycorrhizal partners), one should not expect to find one set of indicator species that could be used for all the different types of old-growth forests. Indicator species are specific to a certain region and a certain forest type. In Sweden, researchers identified five types of mushrooms that indicate undisturbed forests (including *Phellinus nigrolimitatus*, an irregular bracket fungus that is dark brown on top with a foamy-looking cream-colored edge, and *Fomitopsis rosea*, a fan-shaped bracket fungus with a pink undersurface). In Estonia the list of indicators is fifty-five species long.

In contrast, mycologists in the Pacific Northwest examined all types of old-growth forests across Oregon, Washington, and California and came up with a list of 234 indicator species. To be placed on the list, these mushroom species had to be both rare and associated with old-growth forests. The most well known of these is *Bridgeoporus nobilissimus*, which has two common names: the noble polypore or the fuzzy Sandozi. It creates a huge conk-like shelf structure with a fuzzy top surface. One specimen, collected in Washington, weighed over 300 pounds and mea-sured 56 inches by 37 inches. But this large fungus needs large trees. It grows on noble fir (*Abies procera*) and Pacific silver fir (*Abies amabilis*) trees that are at least 3 feet in diameter. With the continued cutting of the largest fir trees, the fungus became rare as well. In 1995, *Bridgeoporus nobilissimus* was listed as an endan-gered species by the Oregon Natural Heritage Program, making it the first fungus to be listed as endangered in the United States. As a result of the presence of this fungus, hundreds of acres of old-growth forest have been set aside from logging.

But in the eastern United States, where our old-growth for-ests are so much rarer, only two studies give us any clues to what our old-growth-dependent mushroom species might be. One is a PhD dissertation by Patrick Leacock, who studied the fungi in Minnesota's old-growth forests, and the other a master's thesis by Jan Houseknecht, who studied the fungi in old-growth Adiron-dacks forests containing sugar maple, American beech, yellow birch, red spruce, and eastern hemlock.

In the ancient Minnesota red-pine forests, Leacock found fewer species of tree-root-associated (ectomycorrihizal) mush-rooms in the 230-year-old forest (109 species) when compared to the 100-year-old forest (125 species). But twenty-one of the species found in the old-growth forest were found *only* in the old forest. Seven of these fungus species were so closely associated with the old growth that he considered them indicator species. The one most strongly associated was *Hygrophorus piceae*, a small classically shaped white toadstool with incurved margins. No common name exists for the species, unless you want to use the Finnish name, Valkovahakas. Interestingly, this mushroom is always found associated with moss. You are familiar, by now, with the association between fungi and tree roots, but did you know that some fungi specialize in associations with mosses? Some fungi even take over moss spore capsules so that instead of dispersing moss spores, the capsules disperse fungal spores. Always more to learn!

Fungi that are potential indicator species of old-growth red-pine forests in Minnesota (from Leacock)

Chroogomphus flavipes
Cortinarius strobilaceus
Hygrophorus camarophyllus
Hygrophorus fuligineus
Hygrophorus piceae
Inocybe geophylla var. *geophylla*
Tricholoma portentosum

Houseknecht focused exclusively on a type of mushroom called agarics that grow on dead wood. She collected 8,199 mushrooms of 189 different species from her study plots and found significantly more species of mushrooms in the old-growth forest than in the younger forests. As well as being more diverse, the mushrooms were significantly more abundant in the old growth. She also found a relationship between the size of the trees, the size of the downed wood, and the richness of the fungus species—the larger the trees and the larger the downed wood, the greater the number of mushroom species. Thirty-four percent of the mushroom species were found only in the old-growth plots. Two types of mushrooms seemed to be indicator species for old-growth plots: an as-yet-unnamed species of *Psathyrella,* and *Tephrocybe baeosperma.*

Next time you are walking through a forest you suspect may be very old, keep an eye out for this mushroom, and know that its future depends on keeping the forest there standing.

Nature conservation has largely focused on protection of rare plants, mammals, and birds, with very little attention paid to rare fungi. There is a park in my town where the county recreation

Many types of fungi are found in old-growth forests (based on a photo by Jörg Hempel / Wikimedia, CC BY-SA 3.0).

department planned to remove thirty-five acres of mature forest to put in baseball and lacrosse fields. Every city council member and every county council member originally approved the plan. I spoke out against it. They thought I was trying to save the trees, but I was trying equally to save the silent fungi. I am happy to report that the forest still stands today, thanks to the many citizens who spoke out to save it. It seems fitting that those same citizens occasionally gather there for mushroom identification walks.

Sources on pages 200–201.

11

Lichens in the Forest

As if fungi by themselves were not strange and variable enough, consider what happens when a fungus takes up partnership with an alga. The two of them together create an organism that is nothing like either one alone. Yet this partnership creates something rather predictable—it tends to be found in a predictable location (like rock or bark) and it has a predictable color (like yellow or green) and a predictable shape (like flat or mossy) and a predictable size (like tiny or large). This has been rather confusing to scientists who like to name things; what do we call this combination? We call them lichens and give them their own scientific binomial based on the identity of the fungal partner. We name them based on the fungus because if the fungus never finds a suitable algal partner, it dies. The algal partner, however, has its own name and can be free-living in a pond or living as a partner in a lichen (in which case it takes the name of the fungus). The more we learn about lichens, the more complex they become. What we used to think of as a symbiosis of fungus and algae, we now think of as an ecosystem that may include a half dozen species or more, including yeasts, bacteria, and additional fungal species.

Many lichens make their living out of thin air, literally. A little moisture and a little sunlight (so the alga can photosynthesize) and they can survive for centuries on bare rock. The fungus provides the shelter and absorbs nutrients from rain or air or rock. They each share what they have collected with the other. They can even host other organisms, like bacteria and mites, and the result is a tiny independent ecosystem.

One group of lichens in particular loves to live in the forest—the calicioid lichens. If you have never heard of them, it's no surprise. Even the geekiest among us who own books on lichen identification may not know of the calicioids, likely because they are so tiny, and therefore so difficult to identify, that the books may leave them out. Also, these are the shyest of the lichens, found in the darkest part of the forest and on the opposite side of the tree from most of the other, larger lichens. You should look for them in the cave-like grottos that often form at the base of ancient trees, on the roots of upturned trees, in woodpecker holes, between fissures in bark, and even on bracket fungi itself.

The body of a calicioid lichen (called a thallus) forms a small crust on, or sometimes within, a tree's bark. From this crust emerge the reproductive structures—minute stalks smaller than a rice grain and topped with a structure containing spores. The color and shape of the crust, the stalks, and the spore-containing structure are what help us identify these lichens specifically. Do not try this with the naked eye—magnification is definitely needed! Generally samples are collected and brought back to a laboratory for identification.

To make this even a bit more complicated, some tiny organisms look and behave like calicioid lichens except that they have no algal partner and they get their carbon from the substrate they are living on. Those are called calicioid *fungi*; but since they look so much like lichens and are collected, identified, and studied

The stalks and spore capsules of the calicioid lichen *Calicium trabinellum*.

the same way lichens are, people like you and me can perhaps be excused for lumping them all together as calicioids.

Not many people in the world are experts in identifying calicioids, but one of them is Steven Selva. And Selva is particularly interested in what they tell us about the forests where they grow. He had some fascinating information to share when asked the central questions of this book: Will an older forest have more lichen species? Do some lichens grow only in older forests? And by extension: Can any lichens indicate to us that we are in an ancient forest?

In Great Britain in the 1970s, Francis Rose identified lichens that were old-growth-forest indicators. In the 1990s Selva used the same methods to examine thirty-three forest stands in New England and New Brunswick. From that investigation he determined that fourteen of the thirty-three stands were old growth. He continued using this method to examine another thirty-four stands, but when he realized in 2002 that the most important indicators were the calicioids, he started using that group exclusively for his investigations. He has found the new method to be less time consuming and more accurate.

Selva has examined forest stands all over the Northeast—ranging from the Adirondacks northward to the Canadian Maritime provinces—and assessed them using his "restricted taxa" approach. For each stand he suggests spending an entire day or two searching and collecting. Originally, he collected from just the coniferous species (like cedar, spruce, hemlock, and pine), but more recently he has included the broad-leaved trees as well (like red maple and yellow birch). He found that white cedars are one of the best species to collect from. The New Brunswick white cedar forests contain more calicioid species than any other forests in eastern North America.

According to Selva's calicioid species index, a young pioneer forest will have zero to two species of calicioids, while an ancient forest will have twenty or more species and intermediate-aged forests will have intermediate numbers of calicioid species. So, yes, the older the forest, the more species it will contain! Eighty-nine species of calicioid lichens and fungi are known in the Acadian Forest (see the list below of fifty-two known from just the northern white cedar stands there), and the most species ever found in one stand was thirty-eight, in Berry Brook, New Brunswick (see the list in table 5 of the number of species collected by Selva at each of the stands he assessed). That finding was used by the New Brunswick Department of Natural Resources as one of the reasons that Berry Brook should become a Protected Natural Area, permanently protected from logging. Two other New Brunswick forests that ranked high on Selva's list were also protected (Goodfellow and MacFarlane Brook). The highest value found for a forest in the United States was thirty-two—for Boody Brook, a spruce fir stand in Baxter State Park, Maine. I am looking forward to a visit there!

Calicioid lichens and fungi currently known from northern white cedar stands in the Acadian Forest of northeastern North America

Calicium glaucellum
Calicium lenticulare
Calicium parvum
Calicium salicinum
Calicium trabinellum
Calicium viride
Chaenotheca brachypoda
Chaenotheca brunneola
Chaenotheca chlorella
Chaenotheca chrysocephala
Chaenotheca cinerea
Chaenotheca ferruginea
Chaenotheca furfuracea
Chaenotheca gracilenta
Chaenotheca gracillima
Chaenotheca hispidula
Chaenotheca hygrophila
Chaenotheca laevigata
Chaenotheca nitidula
Chaenotheca sphaerocephala
Chaenotheca stemonea
Chaenotheca trichialis
Chaenotheca xyloxena
Chaenothecopsis amurensis
Chaenothecopsis asperopoda
Chaenothecopsis brevipes
Chaenothecopsis consociata

Chaenothecopsis debilis
Chaenothecopsis dolichocephala
Chaenothecopsis marcineae
Chaenothecopsis nana
Chaenothecopsis nigra
Chaenothecopsis norstictica
Chaenothecopsis pusiola
Chaenothecopsis pusilla
Chaenothecopsis savonica
Chaenothecopsis marcineae
Chaenothecopsis viridialba
Chaenothecopsis viridireagens
Microcalicium ahlneri
Microcalicium disseminatum
Mycocalicium albonigrum
Mycocalicium subtile
Phaeocalicium betulinum
Phaeocalicium flabelliforme
Phaeocalicium matthewsianum
Phaeocalicium polyporaeum
Phaeocalicium populneum
Sclerophora farinacea
Sphinctrina turbinata
Stenocybe flexuosa
Stenocybe major
Stenocybe pullatula

Selva does not consider any particular species of calicioids to be indicators. For him it is all about the numbers: more equals older. And even if indicator species were known, it would do you no good to look for them while wandering through the forest, since they are much too tiny to identify precisely while "in the field" (as researchers put it). Even Selva doesn't try that. He just collects from many different surfaces and waits to identify them while comfortably seated at his microscope in the lab, with identification keys on the table nearby. This may seem exceedingly dull to you, but for a few years as an undergraduate university student I specialized in microscopic fungi. As much natural beauty is to be found looking down into that microscope as looking up into a tree canopy. At moments, you can get wonderfully lost in that tiny beautiful world.

For tens of millions of years, calicioid lichens have been found associated with forest habitats. We know this from ancient amber. But if all old-growth forests were removed today, many of those species could become extinct. They are tiny little things, yes, but still so amazing in how they have each evolved their own beauty and how they have managed to survive and somehow find the pockets of ancient forest that remain. More of these lichen species might have existed in the past and are now gone due to the rapid forest clearing that occurred in the last four hundred years, but we will never know. You may not even have heard of calicioid lichens before today, but you already know that they should stay as part of the earth's fabric, and the only way to ensure that is to protect the remaining old-growth forests.

Okay, enough of reading about such things. It is time to go out and look for them. You may not spot the calicioids the first time out, but you will find *something*, I promise. A first close, purposeful examination of bark may show splashes of color here and there. The gray-green round splash with edges that lift up and that is a bit dry to the touch is one of the larger lichens.

Table 5. Number of species of calicioid lichens and fungi collected by Steven Selva at each of the northern white cedar stands he assessed

ME = Maine   NB = New Brunswick   NH = New Hampshire   NS = Nova Scotia
NY = New York   PEI = Prince Edward Island   QC = Quebec

Berry Brook Cedar (NB)	38
Grand Rivière Cedar (QC)	37
Pokeshaw River Cedar (NB)	32
Boody Brook (ME)	32
T15 R8 & 9 Cedar (ME)	31
Red Brook Cedar (NB)	30
Little Tobique River Cedar (NB)	29
Frost Pond (ME)	29
Duchénier Cedar (QC)	28
French River (NS)	28
North Turner Mountain (ME)	26
MacFarlane Brook Cedar (NB)	25
Lake Brook Cedar (NB)	24
Marcy Swamp Cedar (NY)	24
Matte Creek Cedar (QC)	24
Mont-Louis Cedar (QC)	24
Sagamook Mountain (NB)	23
Panuke Lake (NS)	23
Brown's Mountain Cedar (NB)	23
Goodfellow Cedar (NB)	23
Nancy Brook (NH)	20
Clark Point Cedar (NB)	19
Rivière Reboul Cedar (QC)	19

Rocky Brook Cedar (ME)	19
Norton Pool (NH)	18
Edward's Woodlot (PEI)	18
MacLean's Hemlock Woodlot (PEI)	18
Dry Town (ME)	17
Abraham's Lake (NS)	17
Big Pines Research Natural Area (NH)	17
Wood's Cedar Woodlot (PEI)	17
Barryville Cedar (NB)	16
Lakeville Cedar (NB)	16
North Traveler Mountain (ME)	15
Hectanooga Swamp Cedar (NS)	15
Unnamed Road Cedar (ME)	15
Dipper Harbor Creek Cedar (NB)	14
Rivière Grand–Pabos Cedar (QC)	14
Gibb's Brook (NH)	14
McGahey Brook (NS)	14
Portage Lake Cedar (ME)	13
Pleasant View Cedar (PEI)	12
Shingle Pond (NH)	11
Skyline Trail (NS)	10
Jack Pine Trail (NS)	5
Polletts Cove (NS)	3

A type of lichen known as a lungwort (*Lobaria*), found in ancient forests of the Northern Hemisphere (based on a photo by Kevin Massey / LGMAPS).

Among these common show-off lichens might be mustard-yellow lichens hugging a little closer to the bark. Perhaps you will also see an emerald-green organism that is soft to the touch. This is not a lichen at all but a moss or liverwort. Nosing around here and there along the trunk and the branches, you may see an organism—perhaps in gray, green, or even dark yellow—that looks something like a miniature leafless shrub growing out of the bark. It is rather dry, not soft like the mosses. This organism is also a lichen, a form created by multiple partners each doing their best to help the others because survival for them happens in community. In some very moist areas, lichens may even hang from the upper branches of trees, looking like greenish-yellow hair or flat-leafy antlers.

A leafy green type of lichen called lungwort (*Lobaria*) occurs all around the Northern Hemisphere wherever ancient forests exist. In countries such as Ireland and Scotland where ancient forests are very rare, lungwort lichen is rare as well. In the Pacific Northwest of the United States, where conditions are perfect for the lichen and where more ancient forests exist, lungwort is much more common. Even there, however, the old-growth forests contain the greatest amounts of this lichen. Why only older forests? One reason has to do with the way lungwort reproduces. Although the fungus in the partnership can make spores and release them into the air, unless those spores land on a bit of algae growing in the right location and not already partnered with a fungus (highly rare), that spore has no chance. (Those of you single folks living in a small town can relate to this.) And to complicate things further, the lichen is more than a twosome—it is a lifelong threesome, where the third partner is a cyanobacterium that can suck nitrogen out of the air and convert it into a form the alga needs. With a partner like this, the alga can make even more sugars for the fungus, so why would the fungus complain?

The most common method of reproduction for this complicated lichen is for small bits to be carried off during strong storms and deposited onto other trees. The lichen even grows in such a way that the frilly edges, containing at least two of the three partners, readily detach in high winds. But this means it may take a while for young, recovering forests to be blessed by the presence of lichens in their branches. Consider the conditions required for colonization: first, an older forest nearby must contain the lichen inoculum; second, just the right storm must blow in just the right direction; third, the forest must be old enough to retain moisture. Once the lichen lands in an ideal spot, it may grow larger and larger for fifty years (some of the lichen you see in a forest may be older than some of the nearby trees). But when all of these conditions occur—which they do surprisingly often—a whole new group of life forms benefit.

In damp older forests, the leafy lungwort lichen makes an ideal place for other tiny fungi to grow. A study done in the French Pyrenees recorded twenty-one species of fungi that grow on lungwort. One species grows only on living lungwort and nowhere else, while another species specializes in decomposing the lungwort that falls to the forest floor.

The fallen nitrogen-rich lungwort benefits other creatures, too. It is a favorite food of snails and moose, to name just two. And the lungwort that doesn't get eaten but instead is decomposed by fungi and bacteria and other tiny soil organisms releases its nitrogen back into the soil ecosystem, where it can be carried back up into the tree with the assistance of the fungal mycelia, which pass the nutrients into the tree roots. Then the tree can grow more branches for the lungwort to colonize! So these lichens and mosses do not harm the tree; they are not parasites living off the tree nutrients, but rather they are epiphytes living off the air and in some cases actually helping the trees by feeding the entire forest ecosystem.

A few other lichens in evidence may also be associated with older forests. For instance, the big gray lichen on the red maple tree trunk might be Degen's pelt lichen (*Peltigera degenii*), a rare species found in old-growth forests. Or the lichen that looks like curvy chocolate shavings growing on that dead branch could be naked kidney lichen (*Nephroma bellum*). A study done in forests of the northwestern United States discovered that the older a forest became, the more likely it was that one would find that type of lichen there.

But we have gotten far off track from the tiny little calicioid lichens, haven't we? You were looking at the bark and the

Degen's pelt lichen, a rare species found in old-growth forests.

branches. You were not to be distracted by those showy rosettes of gray green, the splashes of mustard yellow, the antler-like greens, the golden hair hanging from the branches, or the soft emerald mosses—all more breathtakingly beautiful immediately after a rain. You were headed to the "empty" places on the tree; you were headed to the tiny dark crevices. You were hunting for calicioid lichens.

You may not take long to decide that this work is not for you. In that case, you praise the people who have chosen to do it or the universe that has called them to do it (for I often wonder if we have a choice in such things). Or you may decide that you *could* seek and find these little things, but that you would certainly need the help of a teacher to get started. Don't bother signing up at the closest university (unless it is Humboldt State); the teachers who can help you learn this skill are rarer than untouched forests. In fact, the teacher I would send you to is not even associated with a university. I would point you toward Eric Peterson, who lives in northern California and has created a key to the calicioid lichens.

To use Peterson's key effectively, you would need to know what type of tree the calicioid is growing on; whether the calicioid has a stalk that raises the spore mass above the surface; whether the stalk is narrow or thick; whether the spores are black, dark green, brown, orange, or yellow; and whether or not the spores have pointed ends. Yes, indeed, you would need a microscope and a lot of patience for this task. So few people have the specialized knowledge to be able to identify these organisms that Peterson has a backlog of a year's worth of identifications waiting for him. He will only accept new identification requests if "forestry issues are hinging on their determination." Typically no one pays Peterson for this work; he does it as a hobby, as a service, just for the love of it.

So no older forest means no lungwort, no fungus that only grows on lungwort, fewer calicioid lichens, fewer moose, fewer nutrients in the soil, fewer moments of breathless beauty. I vote we save the older forests—and the rare specialists who study them.

Sources on pages 201–2.

Worms in the Forest

If you are old enough to have gray hair, as I am, you too may have grown up being told how wonderful worms are. I remember both elders and schoolteachers telling me how the worms break down the leaves and carry them deep into the soil to nourish the deeper layers. In the process, the worms create important air holes so the plant roots can breathe. Does that ring a bell for you?

Imagine my distress upon learning this when I recalled my first scientific experiment: digging up every worm I could find in my suburban backyard, putting them in a glass jar, screwing on the lid, and then burying the jar. My intent was to dig up the jar occasionally to see what would happen. I'm sure you can guess what happened. Yup, a slimy, smelly mess. I was only four years old, so perhaps juvenile clemency would be in order, but when I learned of the greatness of worms I kept my experiment a deep, dark secret. Until now. For now, all these years later, I have learned that my instincts were correct and that I was actu-ally doing a little non-native species eradication. A bit of habitat restoration in my spare time. Perhaps I was the youngest conservation biologist on the planet and didn't know it. Guilt be gone!

I still have a clear mental image of the sight and feel of those long gray worms with the bump in the middle (that little girl was not afraid of icky). It was in the 1990s, when I was a very grown-up girl, that I first began hearing about invasive earthworms. Although the story is better known now, it is still rife with misconceptions since the answer to many of the questions depends on where one is standing. For instance, one spring while I was on a walk through a forest in Georgia, someone asked me: "Is it true that we have no native worms here?" The answer to that question was no—at least three species of worms are native to Georgia. But if I had been on that walk in New York, the answer would have been yes. No native worms have existed in New York since before the glaciers, if then. You see, the story of worms is made more complicated, or one could say more interesting, by the history of the earth's climate.

Great ice sheets have come and gone on planet Earth. The most recent one covered all of Canada and portions of the northeastern United States; it also covered northern parts of Europe and the Baltic region. That ice sheet began retreating 18,000 years ago, though tiny bits of it remain here and there and continue to shrink (those are the melting glaciers so many of us are concerned about).

Any land the ice sheet covered has no native worms today, while areas that were not glaciated have a few species of native worms. Given this pattern, most scientists assume that the glaciated areas did have native worms once, but they died out as a result of being buried under glaciers.

In the same way that tree species survived in protected pockets during the ice ages, worm species survived, too. Tree species have spread northward again to cover regions formerly barren, but earthworms are not helped in their dispersion by wind or

The extent of the most recent ice sheet (Anna Eshelman, based on Geological Survey data).

animals in the way plants are. Apparently, dispersion of worms takes longer, though in a warming world we would probably expect them to cover the globe again in, oh, take a guess—tens of thousands of years? A million years?

Now bring on stage the species that has invented boats and cars, landscape centers and logging. We are very good at moving things around, and we have been a big help to worms. How were they ever going to get from southern Europe to this continent if not for our ships? How were they ever going to get from Asia to here if not for the soil surrounding our imported horticultural plants? How were they ever going to get from Virginia to the Upper Peninsula of Michigan without the bait shops and the fishermen? Many different species, many routes of entry; now in areas that formerly had no species of native worms, one can find fifteen different species (mostly from Europe and Asia). And in areas that previously had three species of native worms, those worms now share the soil with an additional ten or twelve new species.

Worms are not the most charismatic animals, are they? Unlike birds or butterflies, they have attracted few citizen scientists or backyard naturalists with the skills or desire to contribute to our knowledge of worm populations. But as more people research worms and learn to identify them, the estimates of numbers of natives and non-natives keep growing. Current estimates are 102 native species and 45 non-native species in all of North America north of Mexico, but that number will likely have increased by the time this is published.

So how do you tell one species of worm from another? To begin with, you need to be looking at a reproductively mature adult worm. Adults have that characteristic smooth lump, called a clitellum, that is a slightly different color from the rest of the worm. Is the clitellum shaped like a saddle, with the front and back extended somewhat, or is it more even in shape? Is the clitellum very close to the head or farther back? Is your worm small (0–55 mm), medium (56–110 mm), or large (111–300 mm)? Is the body reddish, grayish, or greenish? Now examine the sucker-like bumps (called genital tumescence) on the underside. These are just some of the characteristics that enable us to tell one worm species from another. One of the best keys to identification I have seen is the one produced by the Canadian organization WormWatch. But you will need a key local to your area to identify your worms, and unfortunately very few local keys exist.

Even the so-called experts can be fooled. For decades the invasive "jumping worms" from Asia were all called *Amynthas agrestis*, even in scientific publications. Then Chang and his team looked closer and realized that there were actually three species of jumping worms co-occurring in most places. They noted that discovery of these three Asian worms co-occurring was not because it was a recent occurrence, rather it was due to a lack of taxonomic expertise. Those whose job it was to identify these wiggly little organisms figured that if it looked like a jumping worm, and wiggled furiously like a jumping worm, then it was *A. agrestis*. Whoops.

The big question is: What do all these non-native worm species mean for the future of our forests? If those few native North American species had crawled slowly northward for thousands of years, gradually reclaiming their former territory, we may have cheered them on. But any species that comes so quickly and from so far away, and that adapts so successfully, is suspect. Many students and scientists have devoted years to studying the effects of these worms, and many of their findings are contradictory. More carbon storage or less? Hmmm, depends. More nitrogen cycling or less? Hmmm, depends. Fewer fungi or more? Hmmm, depends. Changes in soil biota? Hmmm, depends. For all these questions, conflicting research results exist.

One thing we can be certain of, however, is that these worms do exactly what I was told they do back in elementary school: they digest the organic layer. But instead of this being a good thing—as it was considered back then—it is now seen as a tragedy. The problem is that many forest-floor-dwelling plants depend on this thick organic layer of decomposing leaves, either for the moisture it contains or the fungal networks it supports, or both. After worms arrive and start processing the organic matter and churning the soil, the result is a more barren forest floor with less leaf litter, with tree roots exposed, and with fewer small plants covering the ground. Worms also feed on seeds and seedlings. In one study, seedling survival of twelve of fifteen native forest understory species was negatively affected by non-native earthworm abundance. Some plants disappear completely (like the orchids that depend on fungal partners), while other plants that don't depend on mycorrhizae (like sedges) or that are distasteful to worms (like jack-in-the-pulpit and ferns) spread more vigorously. Loss of litter also reduces the quality of the habitat for ground nesting birds and salamanders.

We don't know what the effects are, if any, on the mature trees in a forest when non-native worm populations are high, but we do know that the seeds from the trees have trouble germinating and surviving on soils devoid of a well-developed organic layer. And even if the tree seedlings do make it through the first year or two on those soils, they are more prone to being grazed by deer in a forest where the pickings are slim because of worm activity (fewer herbaceous plants and fewer species). So although the mature trees may not feel the effects of the worms (yet to be determined), the forest as a whole certainly will when these mature trees eventually die and fewer young trees have survived to replace them.

Studies show that native plant diversity declines in North American forests concurrent with increases in invasive earthworms. At the same time, grasses and non-native plants increase. There is evidence of a positive feedback cycle in which earthworms facilitate plant invasion and later benefit from the presence of the non-native plants.

If you are interested in presence or absence of non-native worms in a forest, you don't need to go digging (literally). Just learn about the historical presence of humans in the area and how the natural habitat has been disturbed. The probability of finding exotic worms is directly related to the duration, type, and intensity of human use. More human presence equals more worms. More disturbance of habitat equals more worms. Near a road equals more worms. Logged equals more worms. Near a fishable stream equals more worms.

In 2015, while traveling through Pennsylvania, I noticed that at one gas station stop, right next to the soda machines, was a bait machine. Just insert the proper number of coins, and instead of a soda the machine releases a container of worms. This must be convenient for fishermen headed to their spots in the pre-dawn hours. But what becomes of their leftover worms? Often, in all innocence, they are released to the wild. A survey done in the Adirondacks found that roughly one-third of earthworm users kept their worms for future use, a third released them in their home gardens, and the other third released them to the forest floor. Only 17 percent of the people in the initial survey had heard that non-native worm species were a problem. And these containers of worms often contain more species than just the one advertised.

My early worm-digging days are over and that guilt is gone, but now I feel guilty about a worm composting project from my middle years. Not the composting of worms, as I practiced in my early days, but using worms to compost food scraps. At one point I gave up on the project and dumped the whole container onto my regular backyard compost pile. Those worms probably still live

Fishing bait is one way non-native worms arrive in the forest.

there as a legacy of my ignorance. And, yes, they are probably spreading slowly but surely. What can be done about these worms once they have escaped into the environment? Few even know they are there. And they can't be pulled up by teams of weekend volunteers the way invasive plants are. There is no known method of stopping them once they have become established.

As I hike through the forests, both those invaded by non-native worms and pristine old-growth forests that contain no invasive worms, I hardly ever stop to dig down and investigate. But I have developed a pretty good eye for telling worms from no worms. Just look at the depth of the litter and the herbaceous plant cover. Sometimes those wriggly piles of worm excrement (called castings) are evident, too. And what about our central question: Are there differences in worm invasion and ecology in older versus younger forests?

A study of invasive worms in Russia found that the worms were rare or absent in pristine old-growth forests. Researchers in Puerto Rico found the lowest levels of non-native worm species and the highest levels of native worm species in the oldest forests. In Kentucky, native earthworms were found to dominate undisturbed forests, while invasive species tended to occur in previously cleared forests. A study done in the northeastern United States (Maryland) examined forests of three ages: young, mature, and old growth. The youngest forests contained the most worms, the mature forests were the only ones that contained both native worms and non-native worms, and the old-growth forest plots contained no earthworms at all. A few studies report non-native worms in old-growth forests, but that seems to be the exception rather than the rule. But, again, it's not always so simple. In 1993 a team sampled for worms in mature forests in the remote areas of the Appalachian Mountains. They intended to study native worm populations; instead they found that 73 percent of the worms were Asian jumping worms, likely spread by fishermen visiting the back-country ponds.

Although much remains to be understood about the effects of all these worms on our forests, it seems clear that leaving a forest undisturbed provides at least some protection, perhaps the only realistic protection, against invasive worms.

Sources on pages 202–3.

13

Mammals in the Forest

Because remnants of eastern old-growth forest are so small—smaller than the home range of many midsize to large mammals—it is impossible to call any of the mammals there old-growth dependent. For instance, female black bears living in the mountains can roam over an area of 2,800 acres, and male black bears more than 15,000; gray foxes generally have home ranges of 500 acres. Even if these animals prefer the conditions in an old-growth forest, they are just as likely to be found outside of one since so little old growth is left.

Small mammals in the forest are much easier to study, but very little research has been done on them in the eastern United States. Carolyn Mahan and colleagues conducted one of the few studies we have of mammals in eastern forests more than ninety years old. She studied northern flying squirrels in Pennsylvania forests. Historically, these animals were found across northern Pennsylvania, northward into New York, and westward through the Appalachian Mountains into West Virginia. Live trapping and nest-box surveys starting in 1990 showed that their populations had declined.

Flying squirrels are most successful in evergreen forests containing spruce, fir, and hemlock that are mature enough to provide cavities for nesting and space for gliding. Flying squirrels feed on underground mushrooms (think truffles) that are symbiotic with tree roots, and they also feed on lichens that grow on the aboveground parts of trees. Since fungi, lichens, and nesting cavities are all more diverse and abundant in old-growth forests, and because the northern flying squirrel range has declined to the point that the squirrel is considered endangered, Mahan has recommended that "all eastern hemlock and mature (greater than ninety-five years old) mixed conifer stands should be protected on state lands in northern Pennsylvania, as this forest type is essential for the conservation of northern flying squirrels in the state."

Most of the research on mammals and the influence of forest age has been done in the western United States or Canada. Research there generally shows that the same small mammal species occur in forests of all ages but that old-growth stands have a much greater density of animals. If all the studies were thrown into a pot and one or two mammals were to rise to the top as the closest we have to old-growth-forest indicator species, I would bet on the red-backed vole and the marten. Although both of these animals can be found in other habitats, they seem to be dependent on food sources and structural conditions most readily found in old-growth forests.

Red-backed voles are associated with coniferous forests throughout the northern part of the globe. Twelve different species exist, and the two species found in the United States are the southern and the northern red-backed vole. Both species are more likely to be found in old-growth forests than in younger stands. They tunnel under the thick detritus in ancient forests

A pine marten in the forest.

and nest in mossy logs and stumps. Like flying squirrels, they feed on the underground fungi that partner with tree roots, and on lichens growing on the trees. When western Douglas fir forests are clear-cut, the mycorrhizal fungi stop fruiting, and the vole population declines. Without voles to spread the fungal spores, no new mycelial networks form, and newly planted Douglas fir trees do not thrive. To interrupt this negative feedback loop, Douglas fir seedlings are now frequently inoculated with mycorrhizal fungi before planting.

As discussed previously in this book, fungi help trees survive through the mycelial network that provides nutrients and water to the tree roots. The trees, in return, help the fungi survive by providing sugars, a moist environment, and woody debris. The fungi then help the voles, flying squirrels, and red squirrels survive by providing food. The small mammals then help both the fungi and the trees by spreading fungal spores in their feces. The trees then help the mammals by providing nesting space. Around and around.

But if you know anything about ecology, you know that something else will be coming along to eat the small mammals in the old-growth forest. Frequently that something else is a marten. These midsize weasels are associated with old-growth forests not just because their favorite prey lives there, but also because those are the forests that provide the large cavities in standing dead trees that female martens use as nesting sites. One subspecies of American marten, called the Humboldt marten or the coastal marten, is found only in the old-growth forests of northern California and Oregon. Because of past logging and trapping, it has been eliminated from 93 percent of its range. Unfortunately for martens, they have a beautiful shiny coat, and trapping them is still legal in just about every place they still occur. At one point the long, catlike subspecies was thought to be extinct, but then a population was rediscovered in 2006. The increasing use of wildlife cameras has subsequently revealed other populations—all in old-growth forests.

In 2010 environmental groups petitioned the US Fish and Wildlife Service to declare the Humboldt marten an endangered species. But the Service was pressured by the timber industry and issued a negative decision in 2015. The Center for Biological Diversity and the Environmental Protection Information Center challenged the decision in court and a federal judge ordered the agency to reevaluate the marten's status. In 2015 the US Fish and Wildlife Service (USFW) announced its proposal to list the marten as a threatened species in 2019. But 2019 came and went with no listing, and meanwhile the number of martens declined. It is estimated that there were only four hundred of them left when the groups filed suit to require the agency to finalize protections. Finally, in September 2020, Humboldt martens received Endangered Species Act protection. Unfortunately, there are many loopholes in the protections and no critical habitat has been set aside for them. After all of this effort, they may still go the way of the ivory-billed woodpecker.

The bat is another mammal that depends on the habitat provided by old-growth forests. Although bats prefer open areas for feeding on flying insects, they prefer older forests for nesting and resting during the day. In particular, many bats use large-diameter standing dead trees. In a study of western Douglas fir forests, Donald Thomas found that bats were three to ten times more abundant in old-growth forests (more than 200 years old) when compared with mature forests (100 to 165 years old) and young forests (less than 75 years old). He concluded that "forest exploitation and management practices that remove old growth and so reduce the overall age structure of forests will have a direct impact on bat populations in the Washington Cascades and the Oregon Coast range."

Likewise, in Ontario, Canada, Thomas Jung and colleagues found that all bat species except red bats were present at higher levels in old-growth forests, and selective cutting resulted in reduced use by all bats except red bats. Their data shows that the number and size of the roosting snags is less important than the structural characteristics of the forest. In the oldest forests, emergent supercanopy trees provide unique habitat. These researchers concluded that "to maintain habitat for bats, forest managers should implement timber harvest strategies that retain remnant old-growth white pine stands in the landscape, preserve snags and large live trees in selectively logged forests, and promote regeneration of second-growth white pine stands to old age rather than truncating age classes at younger ages."

My home is in the mid-Atlantic area of the eastern United States, on a peninsula called Delmarva because it is made up of parts of Delaware, Maryland, and Virginia—the flat parts. This 170-mile-long and 70-mile-wide (at its widest) coastal plain

A bobcat, another forest denizen.

landmass greets the Atlantic Ocean on its eastern boundary and Chesapeake Bay on its west. I live on the Maryland section of the peninsula, also known as the Eastern Shore. In the early 2000s, a friend who was born there mentioned seeing a wild bobcat in the area when he was young. That's not uncommon in other parts of the country, but I had never seen a bobcat there, and I had never heard of anyone else seeing one there, either. I began to wonder if it was possible that my friend had seen the last one.

I began to inquire about bobcat sightings among hunters and wildlife managers I knew. No one had personally seen one there, and they didn't know if any were left. When our university hired a new mammalian biologist, Aaron Hogue, I posed the question to him. It wasn't an easy question for him to answer. He discovered that the previous six decades of data had either been destroyed or not collected by Maryland's former furbearer biologist, and records were no longer being kept by county (bobcats still roam the western part of the state). Seeking an answer to my question and wondering about the status of other local carnivores as well, Hogue and his colleagues conducted a four-year study of carnivore populations. The study consisted of historical, archaeological, and museum research, along with interviews and the use of camera trapping, scent lures, track plates, and mink rafts (floating platforms with lures and track plates).

In the end the researchers decided that ten carnivore species had been present on Delmarva when Europeans arrived four centuries earlier: cougars, wolves, bears, bobcats, minks, long-tailed weasels, skunks, gray foxes, otters, and raccoons. At that time more than 90 percent of the land in the region was covered in forest, most of it old-growth forest. It appears that cougars were the first to go, then wolves. People were paid bounties to kill these animals. The last sighting of a wolf there was in 1768, which we know from bounty payment records.

We also have some fur seizure and fur trade records from the 1600s. The total from one fur seizure and one year of fur trades in the two counties around my home came to 54 black bears, 91 river otters, 495 minks, and 739 raccoons. Obviously, carnivores were very abundant there, especially minks and raccoons.

After cougars and wolves, the bears were the next to go. We don't know when the last one was killed on the Maryland part of the peninsula, but the last one was killed in Delaware in 1906. Keep in mind that the forest was falling during all that time. The land went from more than 90 percent forested to 20 percent forested. Imagine being an animal in that landscape. Even if you could still find places to eat and den, the humans were closing in on you fast with traps, poisons, and guns.

Bobcats appear to be completely gone now, but no one knows when or where the last one was seen. In this study, no bobcats were sighted in more than three thousand days of camera trapping distributed among 224 locations, many of them baited with scent lures. This makes me wonder about my friend's claim to have seen one. Maybe he did see the last one.

Perhaps we will say good-bye to the minks soon, too. A few people claimed to be seeing mink tracks, so Hogue was hopeful when he constructed mink rafts, the most effective survey method for this species. He deployed rafts at forty-three sites for a total of 603 days. Nothing. In the previous hundred years, only one mink had been documented on the mainland of the peninsula: it was roadkill. Thanks to iNaturalist we now have two more sightings, also roadkill, the latest in 2021. On islands off the mainland, four were trapped in 1940 and one in 1975 (now a museum specimen). Small populations may still exist on those islands, but they are extremely fragile. Look again at that number from the 1600s: 495 minks taken in one year from two counties.

Long-tailed weasels may be gone soon, too. The last specimen was confirmed in the region in 2009, and the two small populations left are in low-lying areas threatened by sea-level rise.

So from our list of native carnivores, that leaves river otter, gray fox, striped skunk, raccoon, and (just barely) mink and long-tailed weasel still with us. Six out of ten. Soon, perhaps, four out of ten—unless we start doing something different.

The decline in both old-growth forests and animal abundance undoubtedly happened concurrently in the past three hundred years. But correlation does not mean causation, and it is impossible to separate forest loss from the rapacious fur trapping and bounty hunting that occurred at the same time. It seems obvious that each reinforced the negative effects of the other: as the forests became smaller, the animals had less of a refuge from the hunters.

Although the direct government bounties have disappeared, the old-growth forest loss and trapping have not. With a trapping permit, which is not difficult to get, a person could legally kill a weasel or a mink in that area if one could be found. In fact, no limit exists on the number that could be killed. Same with skunks, gray foxes, red foxes, and beavers. Geesh. Beavers, by the way, were once trapped completely out of the area and have just recently come back. You can kill two fishers and ten river otters a year here. I can't even imagine killing a river otter.

Yes, habitat loss and degradation is likely the most import- ant cause of declining mammal populations, but hunters and trappers—whether today or in the distant past—must also share some responsibility.

To top off this discussion of my local fauna with a cherry of irony, I share with you a story about the local university, where the only wild land on campus is a minuscule patch of native forest. A decision was made to install some statuary to make the area more attractive and more interesting. Look what they have installed: lifelike bronzes of wolves and a bear. The very same animals that roamed this spot once upon a time. Perhaps they should expand the collection to all the species we will not see here again.

If this conversation about mammals feels too geographically constrained, I suggest you do a little asking around about your particular region. What animals were there before and are there no more? What animals are so scarce that you have never seen them in all the time you have lived there—yet can still be legally killed for personal gain? What experiences have become extinct in your community?

This week I have been reading about rewilding and have been participating in podcasts on the subject. People are working hard to bring back what we have lost: beavers in Scotland, wolves in England, cheetahs in India. In a few weeks I will be at a meeting where the topic of discussion will be the reintroduction of cou- gars in the eastern United States. But in the middle of all this talk, I can't help thinking that if we really wanted species back, the best way to show it would be to stop the forest clearing and the killing. In other words, stop the dewilding before we even begin to think about rewilding. Albert Einstein said our task as humans is to "widen our circle of compassion to embrace all living creatures and the whole of nature in its beauty." I have been putting my all into doing what is possible, with my own small life, for the old-growth forests, but when I see these hunting regulations—better to call them deregulations—so out of balance, I wish I had more time to devote to working on that, too.

Sources on pages 203–4.

14

Humans and the Forest

In these pages we have explored the needs of many different types of organisms, from mushrooms to mammals, and we have seen how old-growth forests provide the perfect environment for many of these living organisms, all evolved long before us. Let's now discuss the relationship of old-growth forests to humans— some of the newest, and seemingly most complicated, residents of planet Earth. Do we have any habitat requirements that the oldest forests fulfill most effectively? Are we threatened at all by their removal, as so many other organisms are?

When we consider the ecosystem services that forests provide humans, the first thing I think of is oxygen. It is a gas we cannot live without. Most of the oxygen in our atmosphere has been building up incrementally for the last billion years. Therefore, a sudden halt in new oxygen production would not interfere with our ability to breathe, but that same halt, over a very long time period, would indeed affect humans. Most of the current incremental gain in atmospheric oxygen is the result of photosynthesis by land plants, primarily forests. Two trees provide enough

Table 6. Annual gain of atmospheric oxygen contributed by land plants (primarily forests) in comparison to other sources (in units of 1010 kg O_2)

Photosynthesis by land plants	16,500
Photosynthesis by ocean plants	13,500
Breakdown of oxygen-containing molecules	1.33
Total gains	**~ 30,000**

oxygen for one person to breathe over the course of a year. On average, each tree removes 4.3 pounds of air pollutants while producing this oxygen. In a single year trees filter 17.4 million tons of air pollution in the US, preventing 850 deaths and 670,000 cases of acute respiratory symptoms. In general, the larger, older, and more complex a forest is, the more efficient it is at producing oxygen and removing air pollutants and carbon dioxide. Ancient redwood forests store three times more carbon aboveground than any other forests on earth. And I have been told, although I have not seen the data, that the highest natural oxygen levels ever recorded were in the old-growth Rockefeller Grove in northern California's Humboldt Redwoods State Park.

Forests are also critical to a healthy water cycle, a topic that will be discussed in more detail in the next chapter.

We know we need clean air and clean water, but do humans need beauty? As a species we certainly spend a great deal of time and money on it. Imagine an alien from another planet dropping in to look at our magazine racks. The majority of magazine articles are on how to look better—from hairstyles to clothing to body shape. Think of the fashion industry, now valued at more than $300 billion (and we send used clothes by the literal boatload to poorer countries). Think of all the beauty parlors in your town (and it is not at all difficult to cut hair with a pair of scissors). Beyond personal, bodily beauty, now think of our homes: the paint, the furniture, the flowers. Many people spend their whole lives focused primarily on the beauty of their surroundings. I am not criticizing this at all; I am only using it as an example of how beauty seems important to us as a species. We are not the only species that cares about beauty, but our caring cannot be denied.

The connection between beauty and old-growth forests became very real to me during the years I spent traveling from one eastern old-growth forest to another while researching my book *Among the Ancients: Adventures in the Eastern Old-Growth Forests*. There was always the anticipation: What would I find at *this* one? What experiences would I have at the next one? And frequently, surprisingly, what I found was *beauty*, and the experience I had was one of appreciation and awe.

Since I am a scientist too, I began to wonder if the experience of beauty differed depending on if one were in a younger or an older forest. That's the way a scientist would phrase it, but this caterpillar had metamorphosed into something else, and that something else already knew that older forests were more beautiful. I needed the tools of science, though, to show that to others. So I designed a study where subjects (humans) would be taken to forests of various ages and would judge each on their beauty.

But how does one judge beauty, you might wonder. How does one put a numerical value on a feeling? Here is one way: present someone with a pencil and a sheet of paper with a horizontal line on it; "less beautiful" is written at the extreme left end of the line and "more beautiful" at the extreme right end. Then lead them into forests of various ages—unfortunately there were no old-growth forests nearby, so I used only young and mature forests—and have them put a mark on the line anywhere they like. I did not tell my subjects the age of the forests or anything else about them. After they put marks on their papers, I measured the positive or negative distance from the neutral point at the center of the line, and that number became the score for each forest. These numbers went into an Excel spreadsheet and were subjected to statistical analysis. The result of that analysis showed, scientifically, that older forests are indeed experienced as being more beautiful.

Okay, no surprise, but what does this mean? We know that some insects need large dead wood to survive, but do we humans *need* this beauty? That question is much more difficult to answer scientifically, and I wouldn't attempt it myself. But I do wonder about the ways we are out of whack as a species—war, for instance. What is *war* all about? Why would we want to spend so much time and energy killing our own species? Could there be some part of our psyches that goes toxic when we are denied nature's most beautiful experiences? This idea certainly has many holes in it, and I know that correlation does not equal causation, but I believe nature's beauty is a variable we should start testing.

Have you ever pondered how you would prefer to spend your time if you had absolutely no other obligations? No dishes to wash, no emails, no money to earn, no pets to care for, no obligations at all. If you haven't done this, I hope you will. When I meditated on this question, what arose for me was: *I would like to spend as much time as possible in beautiful natural places with people I love.* There is that B word again. I think it must represent something important.

Beyond what our minds tell us, our bodies can also tell us when we are making good choices or poor choices. The first scientific studies on the benefits of "wood-air bathing" (*shinrin-yoku*) were done in Japan's old-growth forests, where some of the cedar trees are a thousand years old. Researchers from Japan and elsewhere have shown that a walk in the forest can improve one's mood, reduce stress hormones, strengthen the immune system, lower blood pressure, and reduce blood sugar levels. More recently, we have learned of the connection between forests and mental health. In a study of 3,568 adolescents aged nine to fifteen years across London, exposure to forests was associated with improved mental health and a lower risk of emotional and behavioral difficulties. Not just "open space" or "green space" or even places with water views, but specifically forests. But none of these studies has looked at the difference in response between walking in ancient forests and younger forests. We still don't know the full story of the relationship between humans and forests.

List of human health benefits from spending time in nature (reviewed and documented in Frumkin et al. 2017)

Reduced stress
Better sleep
Improved mental health
    Reduced depression
    Reduced anxiety
    Greater happiness
    Reduced aggression
    Reduced ADHD symptoms
    Increased prosocial behavior
Lower blood pressure
Improved postoperative recovery
Improved birth outcomes
Improved congestive heart failure
Improved child development
Improved pain control
Reduced obesity
Reduced diabetes
Better eyesight
Improved immune function

Positive changes to our bodily systems from a walk in the forest may stem from visual cues (forest images to retina to optic

Humans in the forest, experiencing beauty and renewing their spirits.

nerve to brain to hormone production) or chemical cues (forest air to lungs to blood to hormone production), or even auditory cues (forest sounds to ear to auditory nerve to brain to hormone production). This last possibility has gotten the least attention. Consider, however, what Bernie Krause experienced when he recorded the soundscape from a meadow in an old-growth forest in the western United States before selective thinning and after. The recordings were made on the same date exactly one year apart, at the same time of day and under the same weather conditions. Although to Krause's eyes the forest surrounding the meadow still looked the same, his second recording was evidence of a vastly diminished forest after the thinning. He has returned to the spot many times over the past twenty-plus years, but the soundscape has still not recovered. Perhaps our ears can sense the health of a forest, and we feel healthier and happier within an old-growth forest.

If we could roll the clock back to the beginning of human civilization—let's say five thousand years—and compare the forests then and now, we would see that our species is responsible for reducing the planet's forest cover from 46 percent of the land to 31 percent. Of the forests that remain, we have cut half of them at least once. Most of the uncut forests are in places with small human populations—like the boreal forests of Russia and the tropical forests of Brazil. And even those forests are in danger. In places with both dense human populations and advanced technology, the forests have suffered the most. In the western United States, only 5 percent of our forests remain unlogged, and in the eastern United States, less than 1 percent is original unlogged forest.

Although second- and third-growth forests—and even urban forests—are important for clean air, clean water, biodiversity, and human pleasure, what we have learned from the research described in these pages is that old-growth forests have a special role that forests managed for timber products cannot fill. Most of the studies show higher species diversity in the older, unmanaged forests. Some of the studies have found that species diversity is comparable in young forests and old-growth forests, but many species unique to old growth disappear after timber management. Rare and endangered species are more likely to be found in old-growth forests, but within old forests they are fairly common. These results led a Canadian team headed by Mireille Desponts to note that perhaps it is the habitat that is rare, not the organisms.

The Committee for the Conservation of Threatened Animals and Plants in Finland noted that in their nation the cause of decline for most animals, plants, and fungi is intensive forest management. Of the species there that have become locally extinct, loss of habitat due to logging is cited as the main reason in a third of the cases.

According to the research assembled here, the healthiest forest is one that has been left alone. We may get more timber, and hence more money, from a managed forest, but we will not get a forest with greater biodiversity. This is not inconsequential; the diversity of life is being depleted at an accelerating rate.

Some forests may need to be managed for the income and renewable resources they provide, but we should always allow and encourage the left-alone woods, for it is there that our true riches reside. Today, and in the future, these are the places of refuge—for both the species we share the planet with and for our human spirits.

Sources on pages 204–5.

15

Forests and Water

"Thank God they cannot cut down the clouds!" That quote from Henry David Thoreau was an epigraph for my book *Treepedia*. He was comparing the beauty and wildness of clouds with the beauty and wildness of the big old trees. We can lay waste to the latter, but not to the former, he thought. But we now realize that by cutting the trees we are indeed "cutting the clouds." Our deforestation has led to changes in cloud cover and rainfall.

Forests and water are a coupled system that we are still striving to understand. We can examine this coupled system from the small-scale, tree-sized level, or from the gigantic global circulation level. We can also examine this coupled system from the viewpoint of water vapor rising up into the atmosphere, and from the viewpoint of the liquid water that comes down to earth. Finally, we can consider how the forests and the water on the earth's surface interact to affect other life forms. Let us look at a little of all of this here, knowing that we still have much left to learn.

We know that all living things need water, primarily because it is the liquid medium in which all our life-preserving chemical reactions occur inside cells. Plants also need water for the same reason, and because it is a critical ingredient in the photosynthesis reaction—and photosynthesis is needed to capture and store energy-containing molecules. (And, of course, animals also need the energy stored in these plants.)

The flow of water in plants is generally from the roots upward toward the leaves. About 10 percent of the water is used for photosynthesis (which releases oxygen from the water molecule, and also captures carbon dioxide from the air), and the rest of the water, 90 percent, escapes from the leaves' stomatal pores as vapor. This process is called transpiration, and it is a critical part of Earth's hydrological cycle. A single large tree can transpire hundreds of gallons of water a day when conditions are ideal. Multiply this by the number of trees in a forest and you begin to sense the magnitude of its importance. In any given year half of the water vapor in the atmosphere has moved through stomatal pores!

This transpiration and evaporation of water (both from the stomata and from leaf surfaces) creates a cooling effect, because it takes heat/energy to change a water molecule from liquid to gas, and that leaves behind less heat/energy. Cooling is also enhanced by the shading effect. Where there is not enough tree cover, deadly urban heat islands may result. In recent years (including in this book) we have heard about the importance of forests in reducing atmospheric carbon and possibly keeping global temperatures lower. However, much less frequently discussed, and less well understood, is the effect that forests and water exchange may have on global temperatures.

The vaporous water is carried by wind currents. Through satellite observations we can see that wind currents traveling over forests are more likely to produce rainfall. Therefore, cutting a forest in one location can reduce the rainfall a long distance away—across political boundaries. These observations have led climate modelers to predict that large-scale deforestation will reduce rainfall in some regions by as much as 30 percent. This reduced rainfall will affect both crops and drinking water supplies, and could potentially lead to civil unrest and increased death rates.

The biotic pump theory, introduced in the past few decades, suggests that there is more at play than just wind currents in the long-distance distribution of precipitation. According to the theory, forest transpiration and condensation cause low-pressure regions that draw air in from the coast. This moist coastal air then carries moisture, and subsequent rainfall, far into a continent's interior. Forests are key to this process.

In addition to providing more water vapor to the atmosphere, trees and forests also release biological molecules and particles—some living, some not—that act as condensation nuclei. An atmosphere saturated with water vapor is more likely to produce rain when the vapor comes in contact with these nuclei.

And the resulting rainfall behaves differently depending upon the forested or unforested condition of the land. The many leaves and branches in a forested landscape slows the droplet speed, reducing splashing and subsequent soil erosion. A single tree can intercept 100 gallons of rainwater, delivering it slowly to surface and groundwater.

If the forest floor has been undisturbed for a long time, the soil will have more organic matter and greater rates of infiltration, allowing for a larger flow of water into the deeper soil layers and, eventually, the groundwater. Greater groundwater infiltration means a more stable stream-flow throughout the year, and cleaner drinking water. The organic matter in and on the soil (including large fallen trees) acts like a sponge, holding water and very slowly releasing it. More than half the drinking water in the United States originates from forests. Forest disturbance can reduce the mean annual water flow by up to 50 percent compared to that of a mature forest, and it can take as long as 150 years for that flow rate to fully recover after a forest is cleared. Even in dry seasons the streams in an old-growth forest are flowing. By contrast, streams in cleared areas are "flashy"—they flood during storms and dry up in between storms. This can be a problem for humans that live nearby, as well as for the wildlife that depend on a water source. Flooding and erosion are very costly problems in many communities.

One of the reasons that water infiltrates the old-growth forest soils better is because those ancient forest soils have larger and more abundant macropores. Marcropores are formed when tree roots tunnel through the forest soil. As the roots push through the soil, they leave behind organic compounds. These compounds are a food source for fungi and bacteria, and as those organisms grow they stabilize the structure of the pores. Pores increase in diameter as the root grows. Eventually a root might die and decompose, leaving behind a macropore that serves as a channel for water infiltration. These pores are also the tunnels that ground-dwelling organisms, like salamanders, use for oxygen and routes of movement.

Logging such a forest with heavy machinery destroys the soil structure and leads to compaction, mortality of soil-dwelling organisms, reduced infiltration, and increased surface run-off. Flooding may result.

Another relationship between forests and water occurs in the streams that run through forests. These streams vary in form and function depending on whether they are flowing through young forests, mature forests, or old-growth forests. The end result is that streams flowing through the old-growth forests are more resilient to flooding and produce larger numbers of fish. But why is that?

Old-growth forests create structures that are beneficial to fish.

Old-growth forests, in general, contain larger trees and more coarse woody debris (frequently in the form of fallen large trees). When these large trees fall into a stream they increase the "roughness" of the stream—meaning that water now has to flow under, or around, or over the obstruction. This slows the water in some places, creating backups, and it speeds the water in other places, creating scouring and deep pools. Overall, the result is reduced flow velocity, and therefore decreased erosion from stormwater events.

The roughness resulting from large trees fallen in the streams also benefits the fish in the stream. The fish now have a complex "landscape" in which to feed, breed, and rest. The pools formed by trees that have fallen into a stream are favored spots for anglers because they contain more abundant fish, of a larger size. The fish are benefited in other ways too because the fallen logs trap other carbon-containing debris, such as branches and leaves (sometimes forming mini-dams), and this carbon debris is a substrate for very small organisms such as bacteria, fungi, and algae. In addition to removing dissolved nutrients from the water, these small organisms are food for small fish, or for the invertebrates that the larger fish feed upon. Because it takes many, many years for these large old logs to decompose, these stream structures are relatively stable. In contrast, in younger forests with smaller trees, logs may enter the stream, but the resulting stream structures are more ephemeral.

You might imagine that streams flowing through an old-growth forest are very shady places, but this is only partially true. Some stretches are shady, but other stretches are very sunny—in fact, the streams in old-growth forests are sunnier overall than the streams in mature forests. The cause of this is the gaps that naturally form in ancient forests. When trees get very old and very large, and they eventually come down, they leave a gap in the canopy where sunlight enters. Therefore, streams in old-growth forests are not only "rougher" in terms of texture, they are also "rougher" in terms of light. And any ecologist will confirm that where there is more complexity there are more habitat niches, and therefore higher numbers of species. In the forest streams, in these sunny patches, the aquatic organisms that need light for photosynthesis can prosper. They utilize nutrients (such as nitrogen and phosphorus) that are dissolved in the water and release oxygen into the water. These green beings are also both a substrate and a food source for other aquatic organisms.

The Earth's forests and the Earth's water cycle are intimately connected in ways we are still learning about.

Sources on page 206.

16

Forests and Carbon

We didn't always know that trees take in carbon from the atmosphere. Fewer than 400 years ago, trees and other plants were believed to "eat" soil because they were rooted in the ground and got larger every year. Leonardo da Vinci suspected otherwise, but it was Jan Baptista van Helmont, from Belgium, who finally published the experiment to show that wasn't so. He took a 5-pound willow sapling and planted it in a pot of previously weighed soil. After five years of watering the plant, he separated tree from soil and weighed both. The tree had gained 164 pounds, but the soil had lost only 2 ounces. So trees do not eat soil, he concluded; they eat water.

Well, that wasn't quite right either, and it took another hundred and fifty years before Swiss scientists figured out that in the presence of sunlight plant leaves take in carbon dioxide, and it is this gas, *plus* the water, that creates the mass of the plants. That was the birth of the concept of photosynthesis. Photosynthesis was happening all along, of course; it just took us a while to figure it out and put a name to it. This chapter is about other things it took us a while to figure out, too.

For some people discussions about carbon dioxide seem abstract since we can't touch it, see it, or smell it; but for me it has become more real through both experience and time. When I was a student working on my master's degree and doing plant ecology experiments, one of my primary research tools was a machine that could measure photosynthesis rates in living plants by measuring their uptake of carbon dioxide. A typical field day for me involved heading out in lightweight, mosquito-proof clothing, calibrating my equipment, and putting on a harness that contained a heavy battery in the back and a computer and gas analyzer with readout in the front. In my hand I held a clear Plexiglas chamber shaped like a miniature, domed lunchbox. Somehow I managed to get on my hip waders and head out into the marsh with all that gadgetry. When I reached my study plants, I clamped the clear chamber over a leaf. Watching the readout on the computer, I could see the carbon dioxide levels inside the chamber dropping. When the sun was shining, the carbon dioxide level dropped quickly, but when a cloud passed over the rate of decline would slow. Day after day of this gave me a deep experience of the intimate relationship between plants and our atmosphere.

Then, beginning in 1992, I taught university-level biology and environmental studies classes. Every semester in at least one class, I would discuss the earth's atmosphere and the rise in carbon dioxide. Traditionally, we use parts per million (ppm) to talk about carbon dioxide. When I started teaching, the level was 356 ppm, but the next year I had to revise my lecture notes because it had gone up. The year after that it went up again, then again. Soon I was revising my notes every semester instead of every year. Twenty years later, at the end of my teaching career, the level was 393 ppm. Now, ten years after I have stopped teaching, the level is 417 ppm. By the time you read this, I'm sure it will be higher. This has made atmospheric carbon very real for me.

Table 7. Parts per million (ppm) of CO_2 in the atmosphere as measured at Mauna Loa Observatory in Hawaii over the course of my teaching career

Year	CO_2 ppm
1992	356
1993	357
1994	358
1995	360
1996	362
1997	363
1998	366
1999	368
2000	369
2001	371
2002	373
2003	375
2004	377
2005	379
2006	381
2007	383
2008	385
2009	387
2010	389
2011	391
2012	393
2022	417

We now know all about how trees remove carbon dioxide from the atmosphere. And in these days of concern about rising atmospheric carbon dioxide levels, and the climate change resulting from that, we should be reminded daily that temperate deciduous forests in the Northern Hemisphere are among the planet's largest carbon sinks. The terms *source* and *sink* are often used when talking about carbon. Your automobile tailpipe is a *source*, and the tree in your yard is a *sink*. If sources and sinks are balanced, the carbon dioxide levels in the atmosphere stay stable. If there are more sources than sinks . . . well, you know. In the United States the eastern forests are absorbing over 20 percent of the carbon dioxide we are producing, and as a result of the rise in CO_2 the trees are growing faster than they used to. But it's obvious that they can't keep up with our sources, and the evidence of that is the continued rise in atmospheric carbon dioxide. This is very easy to measure, but it seems very difficult to do anything about.

When we lose forest cover, which we have been doing globally, continually, for the last five thousand years, we lose one of our best carbon sinks. An estimated third of the increase in carbon dioxide since 1750 is due to removal of forests. But forests can only be protected locally. And if the local decision makers don't care about global effects, the tragedy of the commons is something we all have to live and breathe, literally.

We are frequently reminded to turn off the lights to save electricity—because burning fuels that release carbon dioxide provides most of our electricity—but we are less frequently reminded to save the forests.

The faster a tree grows, the more carbon dioxide it takes out of the atmosphere in a unit of time. This is true, but how do we know how fast a tree grows? We used to rely on foresters to answer that question. They would screw a long, thin hollow metal tube into a tree and extract a core about the size of a long drinking

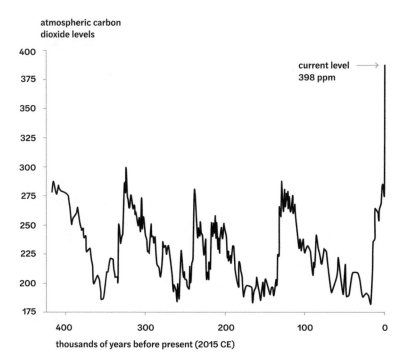

atmospheric carbon
dioxide levels

current level ⟶
398 ppm

thousands of years before present (2015 CE)

How atmospheric carbon dioxide has changed in the past 400 thousand years (Anna Eshelman).

straw. On this core one could see stripes that each corresponded to a year's growth. The wider the stripe, the more wood the tree had added to its trunk that year, and hence the more carbon it had stored. As the trees got older, the stripes (tree rings) got narrower and narrower. This led the foresters to assume that the growth rate of the trees was slowing down. If you are growing trees for money, this is the point at which you might want to cut them down. Remember that economics principle about diminishing returns? It is looking at forests in this way that leads to short rotation times (years between harvests). In Maryland the rotation time is only about forty years now for loblolly pines.

And if trees are growing more slowly, they are taking in less carbon dioxide, right? And it's actually better for the environment to have young, actively growing trees, right? Wrong.

The problem with the former rationale is that while growth rings may get narrower they also gain in circumference as a tree grows. A little mathematics shows that a narrower ring of greater circumference can easily contain more volume than a wider ring of lesser circumference. And that volume is primarily carbon. So the larger a tree gets, the more carbon it is not only storing but also taking in each year. And these calculations are just for the main trunk. Add in all of the large limbs and the wood that they are adding, and you see that the carbon accumulation actually increases continuously with tree size.

Amazingly, it took until 2014 for scientists to document that and agree on it. They found, for instance, that a tree a little more than 10 feet in circumference (think two-person-hugging size) averages a gain of 227 pounds per year. That is equal to adding the weight of an entire small tree each year. A tree that can be hugged by one person adds only one third of that amount of weight annually. And giant trees, like the redwoods, can gain more than 1,300 pounds per year! As trees gain girth around their trunks, their leaf mass increases. So, for example, if a tree's diameter grows by a factor of ten, total leaf mass is multiplied by one hundred, resulting in many more leaves to remove carbon from the atmosphere. The researchers who published these findings (based on 673,046 trees) in the journal *Nature* agreed that the largest trees play a disproportionately important role in sequestering carbon.

One reason it took us so long to understand that forests can continue to sequester increasing rates of carbon even after they have reached maturity is that the model everyone had been relying on, developed in the 1970s at Hubbard Brook Experimental Forest in New Hampshire, was not based on any actual measurements from old-growth forests. Why not? Because there were no old-growth forests nearby to take measurements from. Instead, the model makers relied on theoretical projections. It took us forty years to realize that those projections were wrong.

A 2009 study done in Oregon and northern California showed that if forests there were managed for maximum carbon sequestration (by increasing the time between logging events for managed forests and by preserving old-growth forests), the total carbon stored in forests and kept out of the atmosphere could increase significantly. Studies done in the northeast United States compared many different types of forest management to no management and found that the latter, no management, resulted in greater amounts of carbon being taken out of the atmosphere and stored in the forests—even when the carbon sequestered in wood products was factored in. (The carbon contained in the wood in your house has also been removed from the atmosphere.)

Despite this new scientific knowledge, many in the timber industry still claim the opposite. For instance, in a recent front-page article in the *Lancaster Farming* newspaper, Michael Snow, the executive director of the American Hardwood Export Council is quoted as saying that "once a tree matures it stops absorbing the greenhouse gas," therefore, "there is a greater carbon sequestration benefit to harvesting mature trees and allowing regeneration to take place. . . . It's a question of educating people," he says. Well, it certainly is a question of educating people, but often those whose paychecks depend on ignorance are the last to learn. Choosing to harvest, strictly for economic return, is acceptable in some situations; but misleading people about the reasons for the harvest, and the result of that harvest, is unacceptable.

Because of the importance of our public national forests and state forests in removing carbon from the atmosphere, some are calling for them to be considered as part of a National Carbon Reserve. In the past their highest use may have been for biodiversity, recreation, and wood products, but these days it seems that their highest use is for biodiversity, recreation, and water and air purification—including carbon capture.

Much of the carbon taken out of the atmosphere by forests is turned into living wood, of course, but much of it winds up in the soil, too. This is because the carbon-containing sugars, produced in the leaves by photosynthesis, are being delivered down to the roots and subsequently passed off to the fungal mycelia surrounding the roots, and then the microorganisms that feed on them. Studies at the Harvard Forest determined that as forests age they steadily accumulate carbon; 50 percent is in live biomass, 45 percent in the soil (20 percent of that in the roots), and only 5 percent in woody debris. At this point, knowing what you do about big old trees and carbon, it should come as no surprise that old-growth forests can deliver and store more carbon underground than younger forests.

In 2008, I was asked to be on a committee that was helping our mayor come up with a plan to reduce atmospheric carbon. Mayors nationwide were frustrated by the lack of US cooperation with the Kyoto Protocol, which called for carbon emissions to be held to 1990 levels or below. They decided that if the nation as a whole couldn't cooperate, they could cooperate one town at a time. I thought this was a positive step, but when I look back on our discussions I realize now how much they were about reducing sources and not about increasing sinks. The committee suggested actions like improving public transportation, timing traffic lights, and updating the energy efficiency of the municipal buildings. All good things. But if that committee were to convene again today, I would suggest that we acquire as much community forestland as we could and let that forest grow more and more ancient every year.

As you might imagine, research into the role of forests and carbon has increased in recent decades. We now have a new term for this "leaving alone" of forests to increase carbon storage: it is *proforestation*. The term has caught on, but the actual practice of proforestation needs more proponents. While I watch the carbon dioxide levels go up, I also watch the state-owned forests near my Maryland home come down.

In response to the state's cutting plan for 2022, I wrote, "Recent science has shown that forests are the single most effective carbon sinks of any land-based ecosystem. Eighty-five percent of all carbon released from forest land is a result of timber harvesting. Older forests store greater quantities of carbon, and even more as they age." I was asking the state foresters to forgo cutting just 121 acres of hundred-year-old forest, from a planned harvest of 2,398 acres. The Secretary of the Department of Natural Resources (who has no higher degrees in the sciences, just a BA in political science) wrote back, "These smaller areas of older forests are managed to achieve a greater range of sustainable forestry management objectives, including biodiversity, harvest, and habitat improvement for threatened and endangered species that are dependent upon younger forest stands. As part of our state's greenhouse gas mitigation efforts, these areas are also managed to address climate change, specifically recognizing that younger trees are more efficient at carbon sequestration."

But are younger trees really more efficient at carbon sequestration? The link she cited was not a research paper, but a graphic report. And the references in the report addressing sequestration were twenty years old. This idea of carbon *storage* versus carbon *sequestration* is rather complex. While we know without a doubt that old-growth forests *store* more carbon, what is their *rate* of storage compared to a young forest? Sequestration refers to rate. Some have tried to use the analogy of money in the bank and interest rate to describe this difference. Would you rather have a million dollars in the bank (an old-growth forest) getting 1 percent interest (lower rate of sequestration); or would you rather have a hundred dollars (a young forest) getting 5 percent interest (higher sequestration)? Well, I'd take the lower rate of sequestration and walk away with $10,000 after the first year, instead of the higher rate of sequestration and walk away with $5. The dollars represent the carbon stored, but keep in mind that carbon is not just stored in the trunks. Almost half is stored in the soil, and older trees with their larger root systems and prodigious numbers of leaves—that eventually fall to the ground—are the best at that, too.

The research on carbon sequestration is still ongoing, and there are few firm conclusions. Most of the assumptions that forest stands decline in productivity (reduced sequestration) started in the 1960s. But a research paper from 2014 notes that age-related growth declines in stands are not inevitable. They note, "Declines may be symptomatic primarily of even-aged forests composed of similar competitors, and less characteristic of growth in multi-aged, diverse natural forests that cover much of the landscape." In other words, you will see sequestration declines if you study industrial forests containing young trees in plantations, but you may not see any decline in native forests.

I do hope the secretary in charge of all Maryland's state forests realizes that when she approves cutting of these older forests it will not help the state reduce greenhouse gas emissions. In fact, just the opposite. Much of the accumulated carbon in those old forests will be released into the atmosphere. Sure, other forest disturbances release carbon too, but when carbon losses from fire, insect infestation, wind, timber harvest, land use conversion, and drought were all compared, carbon losses from harvest (intentional logging) were more than five times higher than the loss from all these other disturbances combined. And those figures did not even include the carbon "cost" of harvest—emissions from logging equipment, mills, and transportation of wood. Soil-dwelling mycorrhizal fungi will die when their tree companions are removed and sunlight strikes the disturbed soil. The fungi, too, will then release their carbon into the atmosphere. No one knows when, if ever, there will again be as much carbon on those 121 acres as there is today. I wish we could keep it there.

In my teaching days I used to bring students out to visit some of the older state-owned forests. We felt the relief of being out in nature after days in a classroom. We always saw birds, sometimes we'd find box turtles, or newts. Then I'd lead them to a state-sanctioned, FSC certified, clear-cut nearby. Stumps, tire tracks, and mud puddles were the dominant impressions we walked away with. The next week we'd visit a mill and see how the trees were delivered, stored, and processed. From there we'd go to the landfill and see the huge mound of used wooden pallets waiting to be ground up and put in the landfill. At the landfill I'd point out the flaming vent stacks where the methane was being converted to carbon dioxide right before our eyes. From a living thing, to the atmosphere, carbon can take many routes. And all those routes are all adding up.

Sources on pages 206–8.

17

Fire in
the Forest

This chapter will likely be the most controversial in the book. All along I have taken the information in this book from scientific studies done by qualified academic researchers, but fire in the forest is difficult to study—the scales are so large and the time frames are so long. And add to that the stochastic nature of fire— sometimes here, sometimes there, sometimes intensely fast and hot, and other times relatively slow and cool (for a fire anyway). Now compound that variability with the long time frames required for studying recovery from fire, and you might end up where we are at present—with strong feelings and opinions abounding.

To add to our difficulties, I have almost no education or personal experience around wildfire. For 95 percent of my life, I have lived on the Atlantic Coastal Plain between Delaware and Maryland. It is, by nature, a forested landscape and I have seen prescribed burns, but I have never seen a natural wildfire here.

Some have suggested that I leave this eternally controversial topic out of the book entirely. In the western US, particularly, tempers can get as hot as the flames they are discussing. But my overall goal for this book is to bring the research, as I understand it, to a forest-positive reader. So deep into the fire literature I went. And what I found was that there was no consensus I could discern. Writings on the topic spread out like an inkblot on a folded sheet. Conclusions go in many directions, and just like that inkblot, you can see anything you want in it.

The western US, in particular, is a hot bed (pun intended) of differing options about forest fires and what should be done about them. Iconoclast Chad Hanson says that forests should be left alone to grow old and fireproof, or allowed to burn and recover naturally; while government scientists funded by the US Forest Service are vigorously promoting "fuel reductions treatment" that involve thinning and prescribed burning.

To complicate matters more, there is an economic incentive for some of the treatments that are promoted. The larger the tree you thin out, the more you are paid at the mill—whether you are an individual or the federal government. And there can be financial incentives provided by the federal government, too. As one example, the so-called Build Back Better Bill (currently, in 2022, up for vote in the Senate), which includes $10 billion dollars to "reduce fuels" and another $9 billion dollars for "resilient forests" (that is, money to hire and thin and burn). And, in addition to the financial incentives, your decisions might be colored by fear of your house burning down—and not just yours, but those of your friends and family too. It seems to be happening more and more.

Before we get deeper into all that, though, let's start on the East Coast. The science is no more settled there, but the discussions seem cooler.

Regarding the pre-European settlement of eastern North America, we know from the firsthand descriptions and the photographs that much of the land was covered in what we today call old-growth forests. But if you ask: "What was the fire history of those forests?" then already we are in the weeds. For the past few decades it has been popular to agree with Abrams and Nowacki, who stated, "We believe that the vast majority of the vegetation in the eastern USA was managed directly or indirectly by Native Americans, especially through the use of fire." And anyone who read Charles Mann's book, *1491*, came away thinking of the eastern seaboard as more farm than forest.

But the work of Oswald and his colleagues tells an entirely different story, at least for southern New England. By taking cores of lake sediments, they were able to measure charcoal levels—indicative of fires—from 14,000 years ago to the present. In other words, the entire span of time from when the glaciers retreated and native people arrived to the present day. They were also able to identify the pollen in the various layers, which tell the story of how much forest and how much clearing were present. Beech, hickory, and oak pollen indicate a dense forest, while grass and ragweed pollen indicates open, sunny areas. They discovered that there was a dry period between 8,000 and 10,000 years ago with increased charcoal sediments and increased grass and ragweed pollen, indicating a time of increased fires. However, from 8,000 years ago until the European settlers arrived, the fires were very few and the pollen indicates that the condition in most of New England was a closed-canopy mature forest. Of course, with the arrivals of the settlers all that changed. Fires and open areas became abundant once again.

The lesson here is to pay attention to the science. Many land managers are anxious to prescribe burning as a management tool because they have been told, and believe, that our forests need fires, and that frequent burns are natural and beneficial. But ask these same managers for the scientific evidence to support their beliefs, and you may get a surprised reaction.

In the eastern US much of the controlled burning is carried

out to suppress beech and maple, and to promote pine, oak, and hickory. Why would we want to suppress some trees and promote others? I don't think it's any coincidence that the ones we want to suppress, although native species and important for wildlife, have low value at the mill. It is a problem that we don't know the true effects of this burning. Some managers believe the burning is beneficial for the oaks, but even controlled fires kill many young oaks. Most of the research has focused on just the commercial tree species, and we don't really understand the effects on wildflowers, shrubs, pollinators, and other small animals. Yes, an orchid population may increase due to the increased sunlight hitting the ground after a burn, but what happens to the land snails? When I put that question to researcher Daniel Douglas, he told me that the snails literally boil to death and explode! Glenn Matlack, at Ohio University, says we need more rigorous manipulative experiments before we continue down this road of prescribed burning. He notes that, with the exception of areas near native villages, the majority of forests of the eastern United States were little affected by burning before European settlement.

Do I believe that the longleaf pine ecosystem, once the most abundant forest community in the eastern US, is fire dependent? Yes, I do. But forests elsewhere, such as in southern New England, and the abundant mixed hardwood forests throughout the Appalachians are telling a different story. I am not advising anything in particular here except a little humility. And if you think forests depend on humans to "manage" them and keep them healthy, bear in mind that forests have been on earth taking care of themselves since long before humans existed.

Now let us shift the conversation to the western forests—for that is where both tragedy and opportunity lies. One challenge is that we think we understand fire. We have all had the experience of sitting around a campfire, or next to the woodstove, on a chilly evening. We know that the wood that burns best is "seasoned" wood—wood that has been dead for a long time, and has dried out. We know that the large logs burn longer and hotter than the small twigs. In the morning we see that the fire has burned down to ashes and there is almost no wood left. Unless we have had extensive firsthand experience with wildfires, we may think they work the same way. They do not. In fact, it is likely that fire in the forest happens in the opposite way than you would imagine.

Our misunderstanding of wildfires leads us to see standing dead trees as *fuel*. And whether the tree died from bark beetles or a prior fire, we fear that these dead trees will ignite and put homes at risk. What studies actually show is that standing dead trees, killed by drought and pine bark beetles, reduce fire severity when compared with all-green forests. From our campfire experience we think that green trees don't burn. But on living trees, green needles filled with volatile oils burn quickly and can spread fires up into the crown of the tree. Crown fires burn the hottest and spread the fastest. In contrast, dead trees have already dropped most of their needles, making crown fires less likely.

We also tend to believe, mistakenly as it turns out, that "thinning" a forest (removing a portion of the trees) will reduce the spread of fires. Our instincts tell us that if there is more space between trees then fire won't spread from one to the other. The problem with this thinking is that the space created between the trees allows more light and more drying air into the forest. It is in these open, dry forests that fires are likely to spread the fastest. The thinned forests allow more wind flow through the forests and wind speeds the spread of fire. So thinning alone is not enough, there must be thinning followed by prescribed burning if one's goal is to reduce fire intensity. These two treatments together come under the label of "fuel reduction treatments."

Plantation forests, hotter and dryer than natural forests, act like the thinned natural forests during wildfires. Also, since the trees in the plantations are younger, and invasive plants occur more frequently there (when not controlled by herbicides), there are more "fine fuels" in the form of small branches and grasses. These fine fuels light more easily than tree trunks. Hanson claims that when scientists examined the severity of 1,500 forest fires affecting over 23 million acres in eleven western states during the past four decades, they found that fires burned more severely in previously logged areas. Though I remind you that other fire scientists say his claims rest on shaky ground.

One undeniable fact is that thinning or logging a forest releases carbon dioxide into the atmosphere (see the chapter on carbon for details). And models show that increased atmospheric carbon can lead to the "climate weirding" we are experiencing—including droughts and unusually high winds. John Abatzoglou notes that human-caused climate change contributed to an additional 10 million acres of forest fire area during 1984–2015, nearly doubling the forest fire area expected in its absence. Those who study the behavior of wildfires note that what drives large fires are the weather conditions—almost irrespective of "fuels." If fuels alone were the reason for large wildfires, we would expect the largest fires to occur in the Pacific Coast forests, where there is high biomass per acre.

Dry and windy weather—that is the main spreader of fires, not just fuels. No firebreak can stop a fire where winds are carrying embers up to a quarter of a mile. Yet we remove countless acres of natural habitat and spray countless gallons of glyphosate (Round-up™) in the mistaken belief that it will stop an approaching fire. In windless conditions it might, but most fires are pushed by windy conditions. We may think of a nearby forest as a threat, but in dry and windy situations, the houses are more of a threat to the trees than the trees are to the houses. Most houses are more flammable than trees are. Fires often jump house to house, and not tree to house. There is just one way to protect your house from wildfire, and that is to build a fireproof house.

What about old-growth forests—the topic of this book? In a study from 2019 Damon Lesmeister et al. write, "We found that the old-forest conditions associated with northern spotted owl habitat burned at lower severity despite having higher fuel loading than other forest types on the landscape." The older and more intact forests seem to be more resistant to fire. Not immune, just more resistant. There will still be places of high-severity fire, even in old growth, and I have seen them with my own eyes. I have seen ancient giant sequoias turned to black, never to sprout again. It's heartbreaking.

Predicting fire behavior in the old-growth forests can be problematic. Many fire models use fuel models that rate older forests as being at greater risk of fire severity, because they are higher in fuels. Meanwhile, industrial timberlands are predicted to have less-severe fires because of their reduced fuel loading, while in reality those fires can be even more severe than those in older forests. Some evidence for this is presented by Harold Zald and Christopher Dunn, who found that ownership patterns were the best predictor for high-severity fire in Oregon's Douglas Complex Fires, where federal lands, with primarily older forests in late-successional reserves, burned at lower severity than non-federal forests that were primarily private timber industry lands. But keep in mind that you can probably find a research paper that comes to the opposite conclusion.

There are numerous reasons why the old-growth forests can be more resistant to wildfire. The complex structure of an old-growth forest, with more canopy layers, makes them shadier, hence cooler, places. Winds are slowed by the abundant vegetation in a dense, old forest. If it is a slow ground fire moving through, then the height of the canopy in an older forest makes crown fires less likely than in a younger, shorter forest. Another factor is that as the trees age, the bark gets thicker and thicker, and this bark protects the living wood underneath. The outside of the bark may burn, but the living wood underneath could be preserved by its insulation. A young tree does not have this level of fire resistance. These are all generalizations, and wildfires in the West behave differently than wildfires in the East . . . and every forest type and species composition matters, as does every topological variation, and on and on. Age matters, but so do many other things.

We should also recognize that humans are responsible for the overwhelming majority of forest fires. Some humans start them intentionally, while others start them by carelessness or accident (the campfire that was left smoldering, the cigarette butt tossed out the car window, the gender reveal party . . .). Human ignition is responsible for 84 percent of wildfires. In a study spanning twenty-one years, of 1.5 million records of fires that needed state or federal agencies to help extinguish them, the most common day for human-started fires, by far, was July 4, US Independence Day, with 7,762 fires starting that day over the course of the record. If trees can feel fear, that day would certainly be their most-feared of the year.

When we consider just the wildfires that burn down homes, 97 percent of them are human-caused. And these human-caused fires burn with a hotter intensity for a number of reasons. Humans are more likely to start fires in open, windy conditions, whereas many lightning-strike fires start in closed forests that slow the spread—for the reasons discussed above. Lightning-strike fires also have a greater probability of starting farther from human settlements.

I lived in Southern California for a while, and I know what it is like to live in fear of fire. Addressing this fear is important because so many trees, in so many forests, are cut in the name of alleviating this fear. (People are told that a management cut will make them safer, and so they do not protest.) I experienced how this fear is promulgated when I sent a letter of objection to

Table 8. Home destroying fires and their causes, 1951–2015, New South Wales and Victoria, Australia

Ignition cause	No. of wildfires that destroyed houses	No. of houses destroyed
Deliberate	61	1,663
Powerlines	30	2,513
Lightning	29	843
Other known	35	580
Undetermined	95	1,831
Total	**250**	**7430**

Source: From Collins et al. https://doi.org/10.1371/journal.pone.0162083.t002.

Note: The main ignition causes in the "Other known" category were equipment/machinery use (14 wildfires, 250 houses destroyed), escapes from fuel-reduction burning and agricultural burning activities (13 wildfires, 279 houses destroyed), and wildfires accidently ignited by a cigarette or other smoking material (5 wildfires, 33 houses destroyed).

Maryland's forestry division, after I read their annual work plan and saw that they were planning to cut some of the oldest remnants in the state's native forest. These small forest remnants were about a hundred years old and highly biodiverse. My objection letter was a public document, and someone in the press read it and called the forest manager for his reaction. The resulting article quoted him as saying: "If you did not cut, it would grow, it would die, it would fall down. It would create potential fuel for a wild fire." He claimed that the forest had the potential to become a "huge tinderbox . . . at the turn of the century, a lot of forests were on fire."

If someone who lived near this forest didn't know any better, they might be frightened of the forest. What he neglected to say was that those turn-of-the-century fires were mainly the result of the cutting frenzy that left behind piles of slash in sunny situations. Add to that the human presence—with sparks being emitted from everything from steam engines to cooking fires, and no efficient means to put the fires out, and yes, there were conflagrations. As the rate of industrial logging increased, so did the problem of major wildfires. But that was in the past, and our recovered eastern native forests are not the cause of wildfires now. If anything they are our shield. This situation made me pause to wonder if our forest manager knew all of that and was playing the fear card on purpose—because he knows people will fall for it and it will help him get the cut out—or did he believe what he was saying?

There is another aspect to the forest fires that should be discussed—and that is what is actually burned and what is left behind. As a born-and-raised Easterner, I would hear about the western fires and the thousands and thousands of acres "consumed." For years I thought the trees were literally burned away in those fires. But that is not what happens at all. Most of the bulk of the larger trees remains. The trees may be black and may be dead, but on average only 3 to 5 percent of their biomass has been consumed. Studies show that most of what burns is leaf litter, foliage, twigs, and small downed wood. This small stuff burns quickly and releases 13 to 35 percent of the pre-fire, aboveground carbon. That means the majority of the carbon remains in the forest immediately after a wildfire. It may feel like these fires are emitting massive amounts of carbon to the atmosphere, but logging releases even more. For instance, the massive Biscuit Fire, which burned 772 square miles in southwest Oregon in 2002, emitted less than 10 percent of Oregon's total carbon emissions that year. And in a study by Garrett Meigs and others done in Oregon, from 2002 to 2003, carbon emissions resulting from fire were equivalent to 2.5 percent of statewide anthropogenic CO_2 emissions from fossil fuel combustion and industrial processes.

A post-burn "snag forest" is important habitat for some species.

A more recent paper by Jeffrey Stenzel and others puts forest fire emissions at just 5 percent of fossil fuel emissions.

The majority of the carbon the tree has stored over the years remains captured in the standing or supine bole. And in this carbon-holding structure, which can no longer fight back with sap or defense chemicals, insects find homes. And the insects are eaten by birds, such as the black-backed woodpecker, and the holes created by the woodpeckers shelter small mammals. Many trees recover from the fire, but around the base of those that do not survive are the seedlings and saplings of trees sprouting from seeds and roots. The only thing that healed my heart after seeing California's Nelder Grove giant sequoias, black and dead, was seeing the proliferation of sequoia seedlings at their feet. These snag forests recover their biodiversity quickly—if not their grandeur. In terms of biodiversity these snag forests are second only to the old-growth forests. A burned old-growth forest is not a complete loss. It is still very important, both for its carbon-holding capacity and its native biodiversity. Many birds and bees are more abundant in the burned forests than in the green forest. Don't imagine that it is an incinerated wasteland; it is not. Leaving the burned forest alone is its best chance for recovery. Salvage logging (removing the dead stems) crushes seedlings and disturbs the soil structure. Oh, for the patience to wait another thousand years!

If we are to come to a mature understanding of wildfires, we must understand that these days humans start most of them and that forests have evolved to survive and recover from them. There are big emotions and big unknowns on both sides of the forest thinning and prescribed burning debates. We need to protect our homes and businesses from wildfire, but cutting the forests is not necessarily the way to do that.

Sources on pages 208–10.

18

The Largest Trees

How large are the largest trees in the US? This question is fairly easy to answer; you only need to visit the Register of Champion Trees on the AmericanForests.org website to see the current list. But many of the trees in that register are in yards and parks where the trees have been planted, watered, and fertilized. For our purposes, we are most interested in forest-grown trees. What are our largest forest trees today, and how do they compare to forest trees of the past? What about reports in the historical literature of trees in the western United States and Australia that grew to more than 400 feet? Do trees like that still exist? Did they ever exist? Have we cut down the biggest and the best? Those questions are difficult to answer because earlier explorers didn't have the same tools, the same measurement standards, or the central record keeping we have today. But still, enough accounts exist of our early forests that we can make an attempt.

Let's start with the largest of our existing trees. The tallest tree in existence, that we know of, is a coastal redwood growing in an old-growth forest in California; it is now over 380 feet tall. California has a number of other tree species in the "over 300 feet" category as well: Douglas fir, Sitka spruce, and giant sequoia. Some *Eucalyptus regnans* trees in Tasmania, Australia, also grow to more than 300 feet tall. But a tree's size can be measured in other ways besides height. We can also measure the circumference of the trunk, the spread of the branches, the volume of the wood in the trunk, or the volume of the entire tree. As of this writing, most agree that the largest tree on the earth, by volume, is the General Sherman giant sequoia in Sequoia National Park, California. It stands 275 feet tall and is over 113 feet in circumference at the base. The tree is easy to get to, thanks to park service roads and trails, and it feels otherworldly when you stand beside it.

There is no doubt that California has the most exceptional trees on earth: the oldest, the tallest, the largest; but what about the eastern US forests? What exists there now, compared to what used to be there? Historical accounts of the eastern forest paints inspiring images of giant trees from New England to Florida and westward to the prairie. Old photographs feature large tulip poplar, American chestnut, bald cypress, white pine, and sycamore trees. These images and descriptions lead us to believe that big trees ruled in the presettlement woodlands. However, descriptions of the forests from early European exploration vary greatly in detail as to the absolute size and density of big trees. For example, almost no accounts provide statistics on the number of big trees per acre or their average size. Reports focused instead on the most exceptional specimens.

By the 1890s photographers were capturing forest giants on film. Most likely they took images of the biggest trees they saw, probably existing in what were already only residual pockets of old growth. In the photographs, massive trunks often appear with two or three people standing in front of them. This might lead one to believe that trees of this size grew throughout large geographical areas. However, other photographs tell a different story. Images of thousands of logs floating down rivers toward the mills reveal mostly trees from 2 to 4 feet in diameter.

All we can really conclude from the information available in old photographs, timber company records, the descriptions of the chroniclers, and anecdotal accounts in articles and newspapers, is that old-growth forests of the period exhibited trees of a larger size than what we commonly see in today's regrowth woodlands. Consider also that the large trees in the old photographs often grew in highly fertile locations that are now farm fields, while most of today's forests are on more marginal lands.

From early descriptions and measurements, sycamores are often presented as the largest eastern tree species in circumference, with specimens in Pennsylvania, Ohio, Indiana, and Illinois reaching remarkable girths. We have reports of trees more than 45 feet in circumference from both George Washington and the botanist André Michaux.

Noted nineteenth-century naturalist and ornithologist Robert Ridgway was especially interested in establishing the maximum size of trees in Indiana's Wabash River floodplain. He took many measurements and concluded that the average tree height was 130 feet. He also reported that there were "by no means infrequent monarchs" attaining more than 180 feet. He reported tulip poplars and sycamores approaching 200 feet in height. Ridgway was meticulous, but we cannot be sure of his tree height measurements. He is generally given credit, however, for having measured the largest tree in the eastern United States— the prostrate and largely decayed trunk of a sycamore near Mount Carmel, Illinois, the crumbling base of which measured 66 feet in circumference. Sycamores like that no longer exist.

This shrinkage of our forest trees is not restricted to the US. Large trees are declining globally due to a variety of reasons, most involving humans.

The June 1913 edition of *American Forests* magazine disclosed the results of a contest to determine the largest eastern tree in several different categories. In the category of non-nut-bearing hardwoods, the winner was a sycamore near Worthington, Indiana, about which the magazine reported: "This tree is 150 feet high, after having had its height considerably reduced by lightning and wind. It has a spread of 100 feet and its trunk 1 foot above ground is 45 feet 3 inches in circumference." Ranking next to the sycamore in size was a tulip poplar near Reems Creek, North Carolina, estimated to be 198 feet tall and 34 feet, 6 inches around.

Luckily, we have a photograph of the famous Reems Creek tulip poplar. Another photograph of the Reems Creek tree, taken in 1932, is accompanied by a description that lists the circumference as 28.7 feet and the height as 144 feet. The discrepancy between 34.5 and 28.7 feet for circumference and 198 versus 144 feet for height in these accounts is evidence of the difficulty we have comparing the trees of yesterday with the trees of today. Could a tree shrink that much in twenty years? Or were the 1913 values exaggerated? A photographic analysis by Robert T. Leverett suggests 28.7 feet to be the more likely true circumference. An old photograph of the full height suggests 144 feet to be about right, but the higher, probably incorrect, numbers have been circulated over and over. We cannot believe everything we read about these trees from the past.

The tallest tree in the eastern United States is a tulip poplar that grows in an old-growth forest in Great Smoky Mountains National Park, Tennessee. In April 2011, a team headed by Will Blozan, president of the Native Tree Society, climbed and measured it by direct tape drop as 191.9 feet in height. Later, on a summer day in 2018, I had the honor of hiking with Will and his wife, Heidi, to that special tree. Sadly, we discovered a huge stress fracture in its trunk; it may not be standing much longer. Champions come and go.

Tulip poplar and white pine are the tree species most likely to attain heights greater than 150 feet in the eastern US. It is interesting to note how maximum height changes with geographic location—generally decreasing as one moves northward. In Tennessee's Smoky Mountains some tulip poplars are more than 180 feet tall, and several hundred of them exceed heights of 170 feet. In Virginia the tree reaches a maximum of almost 175 feet, and in West Virginia the species reaches a maximum 172 feet. Through southern Pennsylvania and northern Ohio, and in the Midwest, tulip poplars attain maximum heights of between 160 and 165 feet (although an outlier in Ohio is 170 feet). However, heights drop dramatically above 42 degrees north latitude. The tallest tulip poplar in Massachusetts is a little over 140 feet.

The tallest tulip poplars aren't necessarily the oldest, though. Tulip poplar trees on very rich sites may zoom upward to amazing heights in just a century. Meanwhile, the ancient ones, like aging humans, sometimes shrink in height; they often lose their tops to storms, even as they continue adding girth to their trunk and limbs. So while the oldest tulip poplars are larger in terms of total volume, they are not always the tallest.

The same pattern of shrinking in height from southern to northern latitudes may be witnessed in white pines, too. Historical accounts of white pines describe trees more than 250 feet tall and 10 feet in diameter. Some accounts even assert that pines as tall as 264 feet once grew in New Hampshire. But are these numbers to be trusted? The tallest white pine measured using today's methods was an old-growth white pine in the Great Smoky Mountains measured by Leverett and Blozan in 1995. That pine, named the Boogerman, was 207 feet in height. Following a crown break in 1996 that pared the tree back to 180 feet, the Boogerman regrew to a height of 188.9 feet, before beginning to lose height. It is approximately 370 years old as of this writing. Since discovering the Boogerman, the Native Tree Society has measured white pine heights of between 170 and 185 feet in half a dozen southeastern sites, mostly located in old-growth and mature second-growth forests.

In the Northeast, the Longfellow Pine in Cook Forest State Park, Pennsylvania, was the tallest white pine measured; it was 184 feet. A storm on May 4, 2017, dethroned that champ. As of 2013, at least thirty-one white pines in Cook Forest surpassed 160 feet. All are in old-growth areas. The tallest second-growth pines in Cook Forest are 20 to 30 feet shorter than their older counterparts. Elsewhere, as of the end of the 2019 growing season, the 160-year-old Jake Swamp white pine in Mohawk Trail State Forest, Massachusetts, had reached a height of 176 feet. The largest old-growth white pine in Massachusetts grows in Ice Glen, a glacial ravine in southeast Stockbridge. It measures 13.4 feet in circumference and 161.8 feet in height and may represent what once occurred more widely where conditions were favorable.

Revisiting the anecdotal accounts that claim white pines grew to 250 feet in height, we find that those numbers cannot be verified. There are no white pines close to 250 feet today—if there ever were. It is more likely that on occasion the species exceeded 200 feet in height. Leverett believes that the old-growth white pines that existed in the 1800s and before were larger than what we see today in any of our old-growth white pine sites such as Cook Forest and Hearts Content National Scenic Area in Pennsylvania, Hartwick Pines State Park in Michigan, and the Elders Grove in the Adirondacks of New York State. The tallest white pines likely occurred in old-growth forests with high-quality soils, but those trees are gone as those were the sites that were cleared first for fields and homes. Today's remnant old-growth forests are generally on marginal lands, so we should not necessarily expect them to reflect what is possible for the species. On high-quality sites where forests are recovering after an initial clearing, white pines can reach soaring heights. If their growth continues unimpeded, we may someday see 200-foot-tall white pines again. That's a big "if."

Our managed woodlands are a mere shadow of what once grew. One reason we want to keep accurate records is so we never forget the maximum potential that species can achieve, or accept degraded forests as the norm. Our baselines must not shift to the point that the short and slender trees in short-rotation forests are thought of as average-size. If people become accustomed to regrowth as the norm, we may lose our appreciation for what a species can achieve. The experience of walking among grand old trees should not be driven to extinction for temporary economic return. Even if we ignore all the other organisms, and all the other ecosystem services, and measure the health of a forest only through the height of its trees, unmanaged old-growth forests still win the award for healthiest.

In 1940 the American Forests organization started the previously mentioned National Register of Big Trees. This established standardized measuring procedure enabled us to compare trees that might live far apart. A tree is awarded one point for each inch of trunk circumference, one point for each foot of height, and one point for each 4 feet of average crown spread. These three point-totals are then added together for a grand total. For each species, the tree that receives the highest point total is declared the National Champion.

Once circumference and average crown width—two out of the three measurements needed—have been measured, all that remains is to measure height. And here is where things get complicated. You cannot just walk up to a tree and measure its height—unless it is exceedingly small. In the recent past a clinometer was used to measure the angle to the highest part of the tree and a tape was used to measure the distance from the standpoint to the trunk of the tree. Calculating the tangent of the angle measured on the clinometer, and multiplying that by the distance

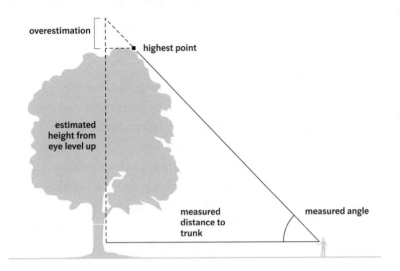

The old tangent method, using a clinometer to measure the angle to the highest point and a tape to measure the distance to the trunk (Anna Eshelman, based on original by Robert Leverett).

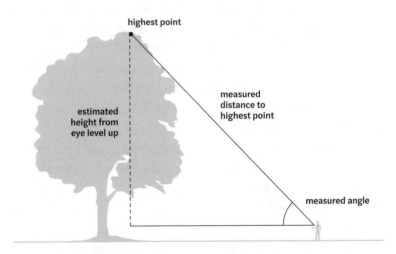

The new sine method, using a laser to measure the distance to the highest point and a clinometer to measure the angle (Anna Eshelman, based on original by Robert Leverett).

to the trunk, would, in theory, give the height of the tree above eye level.

It wasn't until the 1990s that a few tree measurers started realizing the potential for error. In that decade, Robert Van Pelt, Michael Taylor, and Robert T. Leverett developed a new method for measuring tree height using the newly available handheld laser rangefinders. Leverett, cofounder and executive director of the Native Tree Society, has now trained scores of people in the new technique. If you want to become an expert big tree hunter, you might consider participating in one of Leverett's advanced tree-measuring workshops or at least studying the *Measuring Guidelines Handbook* on the website of the American Forests organization.

A new aerial technique called LIDAR (light detection and ranging) has made searches for exceptionally tall trees easier, but the trees still need to be measured from ground level to confirm their heights. Tree measuring in support of champion tree programs is often seen as a hobby, but accurate measurements are necessary to establish what is and is not exceptional. We are now in a time of transition, with some measurers using the old techniques and some using the newer ones. As you might imagine, the National Register of Big Trees is getting a little shake-up.

In an unpublished manuscript Leverett writes, "Where we find big trees in concentration, they are usually in our old-growth forests. There are some mature, regrowth forests that harbor exceptional trees due to exceptional growing conditions. These forests and what remains of the old growth inspire us and challenge our imaginations. We must protect what remains of our old-growth forests and set aside enough mature forestlands to enable the processes of natural succession and forest disturbance dynamics to operate at a landscape level." Just as we should not forget how large our trees can become, neither should we forget that the first call for national tree champions, in the September

1940 issue of *American Forests* magazine, was a call not only to find the biggest trees but to save them, too.

Were there really 400-foot-tall western trees? Perhaps. The early explorers didn't have the climbing gear to measure by tape drop, nor did they have the laser measuring tools we have today. Are there differences in the size of trees when old-growth and younger forests are compared? Absolutely. Can tree size be an indicator of old growth? Yes. Do we want to preserve some forests containing trees of maximum size so we will never forget the beauty and the potential of our original forests? Absolutely, yes.

Sources on page 210.

Table 9. Forests in the Network (2021)

If you would like to experience large trees for yourself, the forests in the Old-Growth Forest Network contain some of the largest wild trees in the United States and they are all open to the public. Detailed information about each forest is available at www.OldGrowthForest.net. More forests are added to this list each year.

AR	3 Trails–Hot Springs NP		Ponce de Leon Bay–Everglades NP
CA	Heritage Grove–S. McDonald Park		Vizcaya's Rockland Hammock
	Pfeiffer Big Sur SP		Legacy Property–Wakulla Springs SP
	Rockefeller Forest–Redwoods SP		Ochlockonee River SP
	Oak Woodlands of Golden Gate Park		Robinson Preserve Mangrove Forest
	Palomar Mountain SP	**GA**	Chicopee Woods Nature Preserve
	Deer Springs–Mt. San Jacinto SW		Original Forest of Atlanta
	Samuel P. Taylor SP		Marshall Forest
	Ancient Bristlecone Pine Forest		Keswick Park Forest
	Bluff Lake Reserve		Ashford Forest Preserve
	Mariposa Grove–Yosemite NP		Glenn Creek Nature Preserve
	Big Basin Redwoods SP		Big Trees Forest Preserve
	The Giant Forest–Sequoia NP		Chattahoochee Headwaters–Mark Trail
	Aliso and Wood Canyons WP	**HI**	Pu'u Maka'ala Natural Area
CO	Hermosa Area-San Juan NF		Waikamoi Ridge Trail
CT	Belden Forest		Kulana'ahane Trail
	Sharon Land Trust	**IN**	Wesselman Woods
	Johnston Preserve	**KY**	Blanton Forest SNP
DE	Tulip Tree Woods Nature Preserve		Brigadoon SNP
	McClements–Fork Branch Preserve		Vernon-Douglas SNP
	Barnes Woods	**LA**	Walter B. Jacobs Memorial Park
FL	Corkscrew Swamp Sanctuary		Briarwood Nature Preserve
	Simpson Park Hammock		Barataria Preserve
	Long Pine Key Forest–Everglades NP	**MA**	Mohawk Trail SF

Rivulet Trail–Bryant Homestead

Muddy Pond Wilderness Preserve

Squam Swamp/Squam Farm Forest

MD LeCompte WMA

Gold Mine Tract–C&O Canal NHP

Youghiogheny Grove–Swallow Falls

Parkers Creek Preserve

St. Mary's River Wildland

Cubler Payne Forest

Cordrey Forest–Nassawango Preserve

Chapman SP

Dans Mountain WMA

MI Hartwick Pines SP

NC Boyd Tract–Weymouth Woods Preserve

Mountain Retreat and Learning Center

NY Fischer Old-Growth Forest

Hoxie Gorge

Green Lakes SP–Old Growth Trail

Ampersand Mountain

Sucker Brook Trail–West Canada Lake

Zoar Valley Unique Area

DeVeaux Woods SP

Reinstein Woods Nature Preserve

Thain Forest–NY Botanical Garden

Landis Arboretum

Paulson Preserve

South Woods Forest–Bard College

OH N. Chagrin Reservation–Cleveland

Wintergarden/St. John's Preserve

Fort Hill

Goll Woods

Secor Metropark

Camp Oty'Okwa Forest

Hammon Woods

Flint Ridge

Crall Woods

Johnson Woods Preserve

Dysart Woods–Ohio University

Knox Woods Preserve

Clear Fork Gorge Preserve

Wooster Memorial Park

Baker Woods Natural Area

Gross Memorial Woods

Davey Woods

Hueston Woods State Park

OK Keystone Ancient Forest

OR Cummins Creek–Siuslaw NF

Cook's Ridge Trail–Siuslaw NF

Opal Creek Wilderness–Willamette NF

Drift Creek Wilderness–Siuslaw NF

PA Cook Trail–Cook Forest SP

Forest Cathedral–Cook Forest SP

Alan Seeger Natural Area

Glens Natural Area–Ricketts Glen SP

Ferncliff Peninsula–Ohiopyle SP

Hemlock Trail–Laurel Hill SP

Powdermill Nature Reserve

Tryon-Weber Woods

Hearts Content–Allegheny NF

Ferncliff Preserve

Carpenter's Woods–Wissahickon Valley

	Hart's Woods		Eagle's Nest–Dragon Run
	McConnells Mill SP	**VT**	Deer Run Preserve
	White Clay Creek Preserve	**WA**	Olympic NP
	Henry's Woods–Jacobsburg SP		Rhododendron Preserve
	Jakey Hollow–Weiser State Forest		Baker Lake Trail
	Worlds End SP	**WI**	Cathedral Pines–Chequamegon NF
	Fallbrook–Salt Springs SP		Muskego Park
SC	Congaree NP		Pierson Hollow–Carnifex Ferry SP
TN	Albright Grove–Great Smoky Mtns NP	**WV**	Cathedral SP
	Fall Creek Falls Natural Area		Gaudineer Area–Monongahela NF
VA	James Madison Forest		Stone Cliff –New River Gorge
	Fernbrook Natural Area		Giant Tree Trail–North Bend SP
	Whiteoak Canyon		Bailey and Burnside Trails–Watoga SP
	Glencarlyn Park		Wilderness Trail–Holly River SP
	Crow's Nest Preserve		Eastern Watershed–Kanawha SF
	Hickory Hollow Preserve		Twin Falls Resort SP
	James River Park		Beech Fork SP
	Voorhees Preserve		Parkinson Forest–Bethany College
	Big Island–Dragon Run		

Source Notes

Preface (pages ix–x)

John Muir, *My First Summer in the Sierra* (Boston: Houghton Mifflin, 1911).

1 What Is an Old-Growth Forest? (pages 1–5)

Mary Byrd Davis, ed., *Eastern Old-Growth Forests: Prospects for Rediscovery and Recovery* (Washington, DC: Island Press, 1996).

Lee E. Frelich and Peter B Reich, "Perspectives on Development of Definitions and Values Related to Old-Growth Forests," *Environmental Reviews* 11 (2003): S9–S22.

Anthony Pesklevits, Peter N. Duinker, and Peter G. Bush, "Old-Growth Forests: Anatomy of a Wicked Problem," *Forests* 2 (2011): 343–56.

J. Runkle, "Canopy Tree Turnover in Old-Growth Mesic Forests of Eastern North America," *Ecology* 81 (2000): 554–67.

P. White, J. Tuttle, and B. Collins. "Old-Growth Forests in the Southern Appalachians: Dynamics and Conservation Frameworks," in *Ecology and Recovery of Eastern Old-Growth Forests*, ed. A. Barton and W. Keeton (Washington, DC: Island Press, 2019), 63–82.

2 The History of Forests (pages 7–15)

C. Kevin Boyce and Jung-Eun Lee, "Plant Evolution and Climate over Geological Timescales," *Annual Review of Earth and Planetary Sciences* 45 (2017): 1, 61–87.

K. Khudadad, "A Middle Devonian Vernal Pool Ecosystem Provides a Snapshot of the Earliest Forests," *PLoS One* 16 (2021): e0255565.

G. Retallack and C. Huang, "Ecology and Evolution of Devonian Trees in New York, USA," *Palaeogeography, Palaeoclimatology, Palaeoecology* 299 (2011): 110–28.

W. Stein, C. Berry, L. Hernick, and F. Mannolini, "Surprisingly Complex Community Discovered in the Mid-Devonian Fossil Forest at Gilboa," *Nature* 483 (2012): 78–81.

W. Stein, F. Mannolini, L. Hernick, E. Landing, and C. Berry, "Giant Cladoxylopsid Trees Resolve the Enigma of the Earth's Earliest Forest Stumps at Gilboa," *Nature* 446 (2007): 904–7.

A. Park Williams, Benjamin I. Cook, and Jason E. Smerdon, "Rapid Intensification of the Emerging Southwestern North American Megadrought in 2020–2021," *Nature Climate Change* 12 (2022): 232–34.

3   The Oldest Trees   (pages 17–29)

C. A. Copenheaver, R. C. McCune, E. A. Sorensen, M. F. J. Pisaric, and B. J. Beale, "Decreased Radial Growth in Sugar Maple Trees Tapped for Maple Syrup," *Forestry Chronicle* 90 (2014): 771–77.

Andrew Larson et al. "Spatial Aspects of Tree Mortality Strongly Differ between Young and Old-Growth Forests," *Ecology* 96, no. 11 (2015): 2855–61.

David B. Lindenmayer, William F. Laurence, and Jerry F. Franklin, "Global Decline in Large Old Trees," *Science* 338 (2012): 1305.

Jack Ruddat, "An Inventory of Connecticut's Primeval Woodlands," *Rhodora* (2022), in press.

4   Birds in the Forest   (pages 31–37)

For a description of the red-cockaded woodpecker, go to fws.gov/refuge /Carolina_Sandhills/wildlife_and_habitat/woodpecker.html.

The Alberta Biodiversity Monitoring Institute's "species pyramid" list of bird species that are old-growth dependent can be found at https://archive.abmi .ca/abmi/reports/reports.jsp;jsessionid=FC2CFB68C8FBF920069A46DE 155CE864?categoryId=61.

Dino Grandoni, "Ivory-Billed Woodpecker Officially Declared Extinct, along with 22 Other Species," *Washington Post*, September 29, 2021.

J. Christopher Haney, "Hierarchical Comparisons of Breeding Birds in Old-Growth Conifer-Hardwood Forest on the Appalachian Plateau," *Wilson Journal of Ornithology* 111 (2013): 89–99.

David Anthony Kirk, Daniel A. Welsh, James A. Baker, Ian D. Thompson, and Myriam Csizy, "Avian Assemblages Differ between Old-Growth and Mature White Pine Forests of Ontario, Canada: A Role for Supercanopy Trees?" *Avian Conservation and Ecology* 7 (2012): 4.

Jean-François Poulin and Marc-André Villard, "Edge Effect and Matrix Influence on the Nest Survival of an Old Forest Specialist, the Brown Creeper (*Certhia americana*)," *Landscape Ecology* 26 (2011): 911–22.

K. V. Rosenberg et al. 2019. "Decline of the North American Avifauna," *Science* 366 (2019): 120–24.

R. Schuster and P. Arcese, "Using Bird Species Community Occurrence to Prioritize Forests for Old Growth Restoration," *Ecography* 36 (2013): 499–507.

US Fish and Wildlife Service, "Endangered and Threatened Wildlife and Plants; Removal of 23 Extinct Species from the Lists of Endangered and Threatened Wildlife and Plants; A Proposed Rule by the Fish and Wildlife Service on 09/30/2021," *Federal Register.*

Jody C. Vogeler, Andrew T. Hudak, Lee A. Vierling, and Kerri T. Vierling, "LIDAR-Derived Canopy Architecture Predicts Brown Creeper Occupancy of Two Western Coniferous Forests," *Condor* 115 (2013): 1–9.

E. J. Zlonis and G. J. Niemi, "Avian Communities of Managed and Wilderness Hemiboreal Forests," *Forest Ecology and Management* 328 (2014): 26–34.

5   Amphibians in the Forest   (pages 39–45)

T. M. Burton and G. E. Likens, "Salamander Populations and Biomass in the Hubbard Brook Experimental Forest, New Hampshire," *Copeia* 3 (1975): 541–46.

R. Bruce Bury, "Differences in Amphibian Populations in Logged and Old Growth Redwood Forest," *Northwest Science* 57 (1983): 167–78.

Laura A. Herbeck and David R. Larsen, "Plethodontid Salamander Response to Silvicultural Practices in Missouri Ozark Forests," *Conservation Biology* 13 (1999): 623–32.

Jacob M. Hutton, Steven J. Price, and Stephen C. Richter, "The Diet of the Cumberland Plateau Salamander (*Plethodon kentucki*) in an Old Growth Forest of Southeastern Kentucky," *American Midland Naturalist* 178, no. 1 (2017): 144–50.

F. H. Pough, E. M. Smith, D. H. Rhodes, and A. Collazo, "The Abundance of Salamanders in Forest Stands with Different Histories of Disturbance," *Forest Ecology and Management* 20 (1987): 1–9.

H. H. Welsh Jr., "Relictual Amphibians and Old-Growth Forests," *Conservation Biology* 4 (1990): 309–19.

H. H. Welsh and S. Droege, "A Case for Using Plethodontid Salamanders (Family Plethodontidae) for Monitoring Biodiversity and Ecosystem Integrity on North American Forestlands," *Conservation Biology* 15 (2001): 558–69.

6   Snails in the Forest   (pages 47–53)

Bruno Baur, "Reproductive Biology and Mating Conflict in the Simultaneously Hermaphroditic Land Snail *Arianta arbustorum*," *American Malacological Bulletin* 23 (2007): 157–72.

R. S. Caldwell, "Macroinvertebrates and Their Relationship to Coarse Woody Debris: With Special Reference to Land Snails," in *Biodiversity and Coarse Woody Debris in Southern Forests: Proceedings of the Workshop on Coarse Woody Debris in Southern Forests: Effects on Biodiversity*, ed. J. W. McMinn and D. A. Crossley, USDA Forest Service General Technical Report SE-GTR-94, (1993), 49–54.

D. A. Douglas, D. R. Brown, and N. Pederson, "Land Snail Diversity Can Reflect Degrees of Anthropogenic Disturbance," *Ecosphere* 4 (2013): 28.

7   Insects in the Forest   (pages 55–70)

Donald S. Chandler and Stewart B. Peck, "Diversity and Seasonality of Leiodid Beetles (Coleoptera: Leiodidae) in an Old-Growth and a 40-Year-Old Forest in New Hampshire," *Environmental Entomology* 21 (1992): 1283–93.

A. Foley and M. A. Ivie, "A Phylogenetic Analysis of the Tribe Zopherini with a Review of the Species and Generic Classification (Coleoptera: Zopheridae)," *Zootaxa* 1928 (2008): 1–72.

Simon J. Grove, "Saproxylic Insect Ecology and the Sustainable Management of Forests," *Annual Review of Ecology and Systematics* 33 (2002): 1–23.

June M. Jeffries, Robert J. Marquis, and Rebecca E. Forkner, "Forest Age Influences Oak Insect Herbivore Community Structure, Richness, and Density," *Ecological Applications* 16 (2006): 901–12.

Erika F. Latty, Shahla M. Werner, David J. Mladenoff, Kenneth F. Raffa, and Theodore A. Sickley, "Response of Ground Beetle (Carabidae) Assemblages to Logging History in Northern Hardwood-Hemlock Forests," *Forest Ecology and Management* 222 (2006): 335–47.

T. D. Schowalter, "Canopy Arthropod Communities in Relation to Forest Age and Alternative Harvest Practices in Western Oregon," *Forest Ecology and Management* 78 (1995): 115–25.

T. D. Schowalter, J. Warren Webb, and D. A. Crossley Jr., "Community Structure and Nutrient Content of Canopy Arthropods in Clearcut and Uncut Forest Ecosystems," *Ecology* 62 (1981): 1010–19.

M. J. Sharkey, "The All Taxa Biological Inventory of the Great Smoky Mountains National Park," *Florida Entomologist* 84 (2001): 556–64.

J. Siitonen, "Habitat Requirements and Conservation of *Pythokolwensis*, a Beetle Species of Old-Growth Boreal Forest," *Biological Conservation* 94 (2000): 211–20.

Richard A. Werner, Edward H. Holsten, Steven M. Matsuoka, and Roger E. Burnside, "Spruce Beetles and Forest Ecosystems in South-Central Alaska: A Review of 30 Years of Research," *Forest Ecology and Management* 227 (2006): 195–206.

8 Herbaceous Plants in the Forest (pages 71–82)

Richard Brewer, "A Half-Century of Changes in the Herb Layer of a Climax Deciduous Forest in Michigan," *Journal of Ecology* 68 (1980): 823–32.

Anthony W. D'Amato, David A. Orwig, and David R. Foster, "Understory Vegetation in Old-Growth and Second-Growth *Tsuga canadensis* Forests in Western Massachusetts," *Forest Ecology and Management* 257 (2009): 1043–52.

David Cameron Duffy and Albert J. Meier, "Do Appalachian Herbaceous Understories Ever Recover from Clearcutting?" *Conservation Biology* 6 (1992): 196–201.

Albert J. Meier, Susan Power Bratton, and David Cameron Duffy, "Possible Ecological Mechanisms for Loss of Vernal-Herb Diversity in Logged Eastern Deciduous Forests," *Ecological Applications* 5 (1995): 935–46.

Mitzi Perdue, "Volunteer Acts to Save Old-Growth Forests," *Delmarva Now*, September 22, 2013. http://www.delmarvanow.com/print/article/20130922 /LIFESTYLE/309220012/Volunteer-acts-save-old-growth-forests.

G. F. Peterken and M. Game, "Historical Factors Affecting the Number and Distribution of Vascular Plant Species in the Woodlands of Central Lincolnshire," *Journal of Ecology* 72 (1984): 155–82.

Robert Michael Pyle, "The Extinction of Experience," in *The Thunder Tree: Lessons from an Urban Wildland* (Boston: Houghton Mifflin, 1993).

Carl Safina, *The View from Lazy Point: A Natural Year in an Unnatural World* (New York: Henry Holt, 2010).

Julie L. Wyatt and Miles R. Silman, "Centuries-Old Logging Legacy on Spatial and Temporal Patterns in Understory Herb Communities," *Forest Ecology and Management* 260 (2010): 116–24.

9   Mosses in the Forest   (pages 83–90)

Nils Cronberg, Rayna Natcheva, and Katarina Hedlund, "Microarthropods Mediate Sperm Transfer in Mosses," *Science* 313 (2006): 1255.

G. G. McGee and R. W. Kimmerer, "Forest Age and Management Effects on Epiphytic Bryophyte Communities in Adirondack Northern Hardwood Forests, New York, USA," *Canadian Journal of Forest Research* 32 (2002): 1562–76.

C. H. Wellman, "The Nature and Evolutionary Relationships of the Earliest Land Plants," *New Phytologist* 202 (2014): 1–3.

10   Fungi in the Forest   (pages 91–104)

My source on fungi associated with old growth in the western United States is the Survey and Management Program (SMP) guidelines of the 1994 Northwest Forest Plan (NWFP).

Zdenka Babikova, Lucy Gilbert, Toby J. A. Bruce, Michael Birkett, John C. Caulfield, Christine Woodcock, John A. Pickett, and David Johnson, "Underground Signals Carried through Common Mycelial Networks Warn Neighbouring Plants of Aphid Attack," *Ecology Letters* 16 (2013): 835–43.

P. Bader, S. Jansson, and B. G. Jonsson, "Wood-Inhabiting Fungi and Substratum Decline in Selectively Logged Boreal Spruce Forests," *Biological Conservation* 72 (1995): 355–62.

Meredith Blackwell, "The Fungi: 1, 2, 3 . . . 5.1 Million Species?" *American Journal of Botany* 98 (2011): 426–38.

K. E. Clemmensen, A. Bahr, O. Ovaskainen, A. Dahlberg, A. Ekblad, H. Wallander, J. Stenlid, R. D. Finlay, D. A. Wardle, and B. D. Lindahl, "Roots and Associated Fungi Drive Long-Term Carbon Sequestration in Boreal Forest," *Science* 339 (2013): 1615–18.

Marie L. Davey and Randolph S. Currah, "Interactions between Mosses (Bryophyta) and Fungi," *Canadian Journal of Botany* 84 (2006): 1509–19.

M. Desponts, G. Brunet, L. Bélanger, and M. Bouchard, "The Eastern Boreal Old-Growth Balsam Fir Forest: A Distinct Ecosystem," *Canadian Journal of Botany* 82 (2004): 830–49.

J. Houseknecht, *Diversity of Saprotrophic Agarics within Old Growth, Maturing, and Partially Cut Stands in the Adirondack Park* (Master's thesis, State University of New York, College of Environmental Science and Forestry, 2006).

P. R. Leacock, *Diversity of Ectomycorrhizal Fungi in Minnesota's Ancient and Younger Stands of Red Pine and Northern Hardwood-Conifer Forests* (PhD dissertation, University of Minnesota, 1997).

S. Simard, *Finding the Mother Tree* (New York: Alfred Knopf, 2021).

Suzanne W. Simard, Kevin J. Beiler, Marcus A. Bingham, Julie R. Deslippe, Leanne J. Philip, and François P. Teste, "Mycorrhizal Networks: Mechanisms, Ecology and Modelling," *Fungal Biology Reviews* 26 (2012): 39–60.

D. Lee Taylor, Ian C. Herriott, Kelsie E. Stone, Jack W. McFarland, Michael G. Booth, and Mary Beth Leigh, "Structure and Resilience of Fungal Communities in Alaskan Boreal Forest Soils," *Canadian Journal of Forest Research* 40 (2010): 1288–1301.

11 Lichens in the Forest (pages 105–117)

Eric Peterson, PhD, has posted his work on lichens on his website www .crustose.net, "Caliciod Checklist and Key." You can also download a draft of his "A Preliminary Key to Calicioid Lichens and Fungi in the Pacific Northwest" from https://nhm2.uio.no/botanisk/lav/LichenKey/Outdated /Peterson/CalKey.htm if you're interested in fine taxonomic details.

M. Desponts, G. Brunet, L. Bélanger, and M. Bouchard, "The Eastern Boreal Old-Growth Balsam Fir Forest: A Distinct Ecosystem," *Canadian Journal of Botany* 82 (2004): 830–49.

T. C. Edwards Jr., R. Cutler, L. Geiser, J. Alegria, and D. McKenzie, "Assessing Rarity of Species with Low Detectability: Lichens in Pacific Northwest Forests," *Ecological Applications* 14 (2004): 414–24.

D. L. Hawksworth and M. Grube, "Lichens Redefined as Complex Ecosystems," *New Phytologist* 227 (2020): 1281–83.

Francis Rose, "Lichenological Indicators of Age and Environmental Continuity in Woodlands," in *Lichenology: Progress and Problems*, ed. D. H. Brown, D. I. Hawksworth, and R. H. Bailey (London: Academic Press, 1976).

S. B. Selva, "The Calicioid Lichens and Fungi of the Acadian Forest Ecoregion of Northeastern North America, I. New Species and Range Extensions," *The Bryologist* 116 (2013): 248–56.

12   Worms in the Forest (pages 119–128)

The Canadian citizen science organization WormWatch displays a worm identification key on its website at https://www.naturewatch.ca/wormwatch /how-to-guide/field-guide-to-earthworms/.

The maximum extent of glacial ice in the north polar area during Pleistocene time. PD-US Gov-Interior-USGS http://pubs.usgs.gov/gip/continents/map .jpg. Accessed from: https://commons.wikimedia.org/wiki/File:Pleistocene _north_ice_map.jpg.

Patrick J. Bohlen et al. "Non-Native Invasive Earthworms as Agents of change in Northern Temperate Forests," *Frontiers in Ecology and the Environment*, 2, no. 8 (2004): 427–35.

Mac A. Callaham Jr., Paul F. Hendrix, and Ross J. Phillips. "Occurrence of an Exotic Earthworm (*Amynthas agrestis*) in Undisturbed Soils of the Southern Appalachian Mountains, USA," *Pedobiologia* 47, nos. 5/6 (2004): 466–70.

C. H. Chang, K. Szlavecz, M. R. Johnston, J. H. Gorres, A. Davalos, and D. McHugh, "Co-Invasion of Three Asian Earthworms, *Metaphire hilgendorfi*, *Amynthas agrestis* and *Amynthas tokioensis* in the USA," *Biological Invasions* 20, no. 4 (2018): 843–48.

Chih-Han Chang, Marie L. C. Bartz, George Brown, Mac A. Callaham, Erin K. Cameron, Andrea Dávalos, Annise Dobson, et al. "The Second Wave of Earthworm Invasions in North America: Biology, Environmental Impacts, Management and Control of Invasive Jumping Worms," *Biological Invasions* 23, no. 11 (2021): 3291–3322.

D. Craven, M. P. Thakur, E. K. Cameron, L. E. Frelich, R. Beauséjour, R. B. Blair, B. Blossey, et al., "The Unseen Invaders: Introduced Earthworms as Drivers of Change in Plant Communities in North American Forests (a Meta-analysis)," *Global Change Biology* 23 (2017): 1065–74.

A. Dobson and B. Blossey, "Earthworm Invasion, White-tailed Deer and Seedling Establishment in Deciduous Forests of North-Eastern North America," *Journal of Ecology* 103 (2015): 153–64.

Lee E. Frelich, Bernd Blossey, Erin K Cameron, Andrea Dávalos, Nico Eisenhauer, Timothy Fahey, Olga Ferlian, et al. "Side-Swiped: Ecological Cascades Emanating from Earthworm Invasions," *Frontiers in Ecology and the Environment* 17, no. 9 (2019): 502–10.

C. M. Hale, L. E. Frelich, and P. B. Reich, "Exotic European Earthworm Invasion Dynamics in Northern Hardwood Forests of Minnesota, USA," *Ecological Applications* 15 (2005): 848–60.

Paul F. Hendrix, Mac A. Callaham, John M. Drake, Ching-Yu Huang, Sam W. James, Bruce A. Snyder, and Weixin Zhang, "Pandora's Box Contained Bait: The Global Problem of Introduced Earthworms," *Annual Review of Ecology, Evolution, and Systematics* 39 (2008): 593–613.

P. J. Kalisz and D. B. Dotson, "Land-Use History and the Occurrence of Exotic Earthworms in the Mountains of Eastern Kentucky," *American Midland Naturalist* 122 (1989): 288–97.

Y. Sanchez-de Leon, X. Zou, S. Borges, and H. Ruan, "Recovery of Native Earthworms in Abandoned Tropical Pastures," *Conservation Biology* 17 (2003): 999–1006.

Dara E. Seidl and Peter Klepeis, "Human Dimensions of Earthworm Invasion in the Adirondack State Park," *Human Ecology* 39 (2011): 641–55.

Katalin Szlávecz and Csaba Csuzdi, "Land Use Change Affects Earthworm Communities in Eastern Maryland, USA," *European Journal of Soil Biology* 43, Suppl. 1 (2007): S79–S85.

Alexei V. Tiunov, Cindy M. Hale, Andrew R. Holdsworth, and Tamara S. Vsevolodova-Perel, "Invasion Patterns of Lumbricidae into the Previously Earthworm-Free Areas of Northeastern Europe and the Western Great Lakes Region of North America," *Biological Invasions* 8 (2006): 1223–34.

13   Mammals in the Forest   (pages 129–138)

Current Maryland trapping regulations can be found at the Maryland Guide to Hunting & Trapping site at https://www.eregulations.com/maryland /hunting/furbearer-hunting-trapping.

My source about black bear range is the Northwest Wildlife Preservation Society's species report on black bears, accessible at https://northwest wildlife.com/species-reports/.

Facts about foxes found in New Jersey can be viewed on the New Jersey Division of Fish and Wildlife website at https://state.nj.us/dep/fgw /speciesinfo_fox.htm.

A. B. Carey and M. L. Johnson, "Small Mammals in Managed, Naturally Young, and Old-Growth Forests," *Ecological Applications* 5 (1995): 336–52.

Aaron Hogue, "Mammalian Carnivore Decline on the Delmarva Peninsula," *Maryland Naturalist* 53 (2015): 2–33.

Thomas S. Jung, Ian D. Thompson, Rodger D. Titman, and Andrew P. Applejohn, "Habitat Selection by Forest Bats in Relation to Mixed-Wood Stand Types and Structure in Central Ontario," *Journal of Wildlife Management* 63 (1999): 1306–19.

C. G. Mahan, J. A. Bishop, M. A. Steele, G. Turner, and W. L. Myers, "Habitat Characteristics and Revised Gap Landscape Analysis for the Northern Flying Squirrel (*Glaucomys sabrinus*), a State Endangered Species in Pennsylvania," *American Midland Naturalist* 164 (2010): 283–95.

Carolyn G. Mahan, Michael A. Steele, Michael J. Patrick, et al., "The Status of the Northern Flying Squirrel (*Glaucomys sabrinus*) in Pennsylvania," *Journal of the Pennsylvania Academy of Science* 73 (1999): 15–21.

T. P. Sullivan, D. S. Sullivan, P. M. F. Lindgren, and D. B. Ransome, 2009. "Stand Structure and the Abundance and Diversity of Plants and Small Mammals in Natural and Intensively Managed Forests," *Forest Ecology and Management* 258S (2009): S127–S141.

Thomas P. Sullivan, Druscilla S. Sullivan, Pontus M. F. Lindgren, and Douglas B. Ransome, "If We Build Habitat, Will They Come? Woody Debris Structures and Conservation of Forest Mammals," *Journal of Mammalogy* 93 (2012): 1456–68.

D. Thomas, "The Distribution of Bats in Different Ages of Douglas-Fir Forests," *Journal of Wildlife Management* 52 (1988): 619–26.

14 Humans and the Forest (pages 139–148)

Information on the oxygen cycle came from *New World Encyclopedia*, "Biogeochemical cycle" entry, at https://newworldencyclopedia.org/p/index.php?title=Biogeochemical_cycle&oldid=977476.

G. Bratman et al., "Nature and Mental Health: An Ecosystem Service Perspective," *Science Advances* 5, no. 7 (2019).

R. T. Buxton, A. L.Pearson, C. Allou, K. Fristrup, G. Wittemyer, "A Synthesis of Health Benefits of Natural Sounds and Their Distribution in National Parks," *Proceedings of the National Academy of Sciences* 118 (2021): e2013097118.

M. Desponts, G. Brunet, L. Bélanger, and M. Bouchard, "The Eastern Boreal Old-Growth Balsam Fir Forest: A Distinct Ecosystem," *Canadian Journal of Botany* 82 (2004): 830–49.

H. Frumkin, G. N. Bratman, S. J. Breslow, et al. "Nature Contact and Human Health: A Research Agenda." *Environmental Health Perspectives*, 125, no. 7 (2017): 1–18.

V. Goold, S. Horsley, and J. Maloof, "Vitamin F: Forests Are Critical for Human and Planetary Health," an online publication of the *Old-Growth Forest Network* (2021), https://www.oldgrowthforest.net.

Daniela Haluza, Regina Schönbauer, and Renate Cervinka, "Green Perspectives for Public Health: A Narrative Review on the Physiological Effects of Experiencing Outdoor Nature," *International Journal of Environmental Research and Public Health* 11 (2014): 5445–61.

Bernie Krause, *The Great Animal Orchestra* (Boston: Little, Brown, 2012). The anecdote I cite is from pages 68–71.

M. J. A. Maes, M. Pirani, E. R. Booth, et al. "Benefit of Woodland and Other Natural Environments for Adolescents' Cognition and Mental Health," *Nature Sustainability* 4 (2021): 851–58.

Joan Maloof, "Measuring the Beauty of Forests," *International Journal of Environmental Studies* 67 (2010): 431–37.

K. Meyer and R. Bürger-Arndt, "How Forests Foster Human Health—Present State of Research-Based Knowledge (in the Field of Forests and Human Health)," *International Forestry Review* 16 (2014): 421–46.

K. N. Ninan and Makoto Inoue, "Valuing Forest Ecosystem Services: What We Know and What We Don't," *Ecological Economics* 93 (2013): 137–49.

B. J. Park, Y. Tsunetsugu, T. Kasetani, T. Kagawa, and Y. Miyazaki, "The Physiological Effects of Shinrin-yoku (Taking in the Forest Atmosphere or Forest Bathing): Evidence from Field Experiments in 24 Forests across Japan," *Environmental Health and Preventive Medicine* 15 (2010): 18–26.

Pertti Rassi and Rauno Väisänen, eds., *Threatened Animals and Plants in Finland: English Summary of the Report of the Committee for the Conservation of Threatened Animals and Plants in Finland* (Helsinki: Ympäristöministeriö, 1987).

US Department of Agriculture, Forest Service. FS-1096. Washington, DC (2018).

15 Forests and Water (pages 149–155)

Nicole A. L. Archer, Wilfred Otten, Sonja Schmidt, A. Glyn Bengough, Nadeem Shah, and Mike Bonell, "Rainfall Infiltration and Soil Hydrological Characteristics below Ancient Forest, Planted Forest and Grassland in a Temperate Northern Climate: Influence of Forest Age on Rainfall Infiltration in Temperate Environments," *Ecohydrology* 9, no. 4 (2016): 585–600.

David Ellison, Cindy E. Morris, Bruno Locatelli, Douglas Sheil, Jane Cohen, Daniel Murdiyarso, Victoria Gutierrez, et al., "Trees, Forests and Water: Cool Insights for a Hot World." *Global Environmental Change: Human and Policy Dimensions* 43 (2017): 51–61.

M. D. A. Jayasuriya, G. Dunn, R. Benyon, and P. J. O'Shaughnessy, "Some Factors Affecting Water Yield from Mountain Ash (*Eucalyptus regnans*) Dominated Forests in South-East Australia," *Journal of Hydrology* 150 (1993): 345–67.

Daniel G. Neary, George G. Ice, and C. Rhett Jackson, "Linkages between Forest Soils and Water Quality and Quantity," *Forest Ecology and Management* 258, no. 10 (2009): 2269–81.

D. R. Warren, W. S. Keeton, H. A. Bechtold, C. E. Kraft, "Forest-Stream Interactions in Eastern Old-Growth Forests," in *Ecology and Recovery of Eastern Old-Growth Forests*, edited by A. M. Barton and W. S. Keeton (Washington DC: Island Press, 2018).

16 Forests and Carbon (pages 157–167)

Data on ppm of CO_2 in the atmosphere are from CO2Now.org.

K. E. Clemmensen, A. Bahr, O. Ovaskainen, A. Dahlberg, A. Ekblad, H. Wallander, J. Stenlid, R. D. Finlay, D. A. Wardle, and B. D. Lindahl, "Roots and Associated Fungi Drive Long-Term Carbon Sequestration in Boreal Forest," *Science*, New Series, 339 (2013): 1615–18.

A. C. Finzi, M. Giasson, A. A. Barker Plotkin, J. D. Aber, E. R. Boose, E. A. Davidson, M. C. Dietze, et al., "Carbon Budget of the Harvard Forest Long-Term Ecological Research Site: Pattern, Process, and Response to Global Change," *Ecological Monographs* 90, no. 4 (2020). https://doi:10.1002/ecm.1423.

Jane R. Foster, Anthony W. D'Amato, and John B Bradford. "Looking for Age-Related Growth Decline in Natural Forests: Unexpected Biomass Patterns from Tree Rings and Simulated Mortality," *Oecologia* 175, no. 1 (2014): 363–74.

B. W. Griscom, J. Adams, et al., "Natural Climate Solutions," *Proceedings of the National Academy of Sciences* 114 (2017): 11645–50.

N. L. Harris et al. "Attribution of Net Carbon Change by Disturbance Type across Forest Lands of the Conterminous United States," *Carbon Balance Management* 11 (2016): 24.

Tara W. Hudiburg, Beverly E. Law, William R. Moomaw, Mark E. Harmon, and Jeffrey E. Stenzel, "Meeting GHG Reduction Targets Requires Accounting for All Forest Sector Emissions," *Environmental Research Letters* 14, no. 9 (2019): 095005.

Tara Hudiburg, Beverly Law, David P. Turner, John Campbell, Dan Donato, and Maureen Duane, "Carbon Dynamics of Oregon and Northern California Forests and Potential Land-Based Carbon Storage," *Ecological Applications* 19 (2009): 163–80.

T. Klein et al., "Belowground Carbon Trade among Tall Trees in a Temperate Forest," *Science* 352 (2016): 342–44.

Robert T. Leverett, Susan A. Masino, William Moomaw, "Older Eastern White Pine Trees and Stands Accumulate Carbon for Many Decades and Maximize Cumulative Carbon," *Frontiers in Forests and Global Change* 4 (2021): 1–12.

J. A. Lutz et al., "Global Importance of Large-Diameter Trees," *Global Ecology and Biogeography* 27, no. 7 (2018): 849–64.

S. Luyssaert et al., "Old-Growth Forests as Global Carbon Sinks," *Nature* 455 (2008): 213–15.

D. C. McKinley et al., "A Synthesis of Current Knowledge on Forests and Carbon Storage in the United States," *Ecological Applications* 21, no. 6 (2011): 1902–24.

W. R. Moomaw, S. A. Masino, and E. K. Faison, "Intact Forests in the United States: Proforestation Mitigates Climate Change and Serves the Greatest Good," *Frontiers in Forests and Global Change* 2 (2019): 1–27.

Elly Morrien et al., "Soil Networks Become More Connected and Take Up More Carbon as Nature Restoration Progresses," *Nature Communications* 8 (2017): 14349.

Jared S. Nunery and William S. Keeton, "Forest Carbon Storage in the Northeastern United States: Net Effects of Harvesting Frequency, Post-Harvest Retention, and Wood Products," *Forest Ecology and Management* 259 (2010): 1363–75.

Stephen C. Sillett, Robert Van Pelt, George W. Koch, Anthony R. Ambrose, Allyson L. Carroll, Marie E. Antoine, and Brett M. Mifsud, "Increasing Wood Production through Old Age in Tall Trees," *Forest Ecology and Management* 259 (2010): 976–94.

N. L. Stephenson, A. J. Das, R. Condit, S. E. Russo, P. J. Baker, N. G. Beckman, D. A. Coomes, et al., "Rate of Tree Carbon Accumulation Increases Continuously with Tree Size," *Nature* 507 (2014): 90–93.

Tom Venesky, "Misconception Makes Hardwood a Hard Sell in the US: Pennsylvania Timber Industry Prioritizes its Environmental Message," *Lancaster Farming* 67, no. 8 (November 20, 2021): 1.

G. Zhou et al., "Old-Growth Forests Can Accumulate Carbon in Soils," *Science* 314, no. 1 (2006): 1417.

17   Fire in the Forest   (pages 169–180)

John T. Abatzoglou and A. Park Williams, "Impact of Anthropogenic Climate Change on Wildfire across Western US Forests," *Proceedings of the National Academy of Sciences* 113, no. 42 (2016): 11770–75.

Jennifer K. Balch, Bethany A. Bradley, John T. Abatzoglou, R. Chelsea Nagy, Emily J. Fusco, Adam L. Mahood, "Human-Started Wildfires Expand the Fire Niche across the United States," *Proceedings of the National Academy of Sciences* 114, no. 11 (2017): 2946–29.

Carl E. Bock and James F Lynch, "Breeding Bird Populations of Burned and Unburned Conifer Forest in the Sierra Nevada," *The Condor* 72, no. 2 (1970): 182–89.

Monica Bond, Derek E. Lee, Curtis M. Bradley, and Chad T. Hanson, "Influence of Pre-Fire Tree Mortality on Fire Severity in Conifer Forests of the San Bernardino Mountains, California," *Open Forest Science Journal* 2, no. 1 (2009): 41–47.

K. M. Collins, T. D. Penman, and O. F. Price, "Some Wildfire Ignition Causes Pose More Risk of Destroying Houses than Others," *PLoS One* 11, no. 9 (2016): e0162083.

Sara M. Galbraith, James H. Cane, Andrew R. Moldenke, and James W. Rivers, "Wild Bee Diversity Increases with Local Fire Severity in a Fire-Prone Landscape." *Ecosphere* 10, no. 4 (2019).

Chad Hanson, *Smokescreen: Debunking Wildfire Myths to Save Our Forests and Our Climate* (Lexington, KY: University Press of Kentucky, 2021).

Beverly E. Law, Tara W. Hudiburg, Logan T. Berner, Jeffrey J. Kent, Polly C. Buotte, Mark E. Harmon, "Land Use Strategies to Mitigate Climate Change in Carbon Dense Temperate Forests," *Proceedings of the National Academy of Sciences*, 115, no. 14 (2018): 3663–68.

D. B. Lesmeister, R. J. Davis, S. G. Sovern, et al., "Northern Spotted Owl Nesting Forests as Fire Refugia: A 30-Year Synthesis of Large Wildfires," *Fire Ecology*, 17, no. 32 (2021): 1–18.

D. B. Lesmeister, S. G. Sovern, R. J. Davis, D. M. Bell, M. J. Gregory, and J. C. Vogele, "Mixed-Severity Wildfire and Habitat of an Old-Forest Obligate," *Ecosphere* 10, no. 4 (2019): e02696.

Glen R. Matlack, "Reassessment of the Use of Fire as a Management Tool in Deciduous Forests of Eastern North America," *Conservation Biology* 27, no. 5 (2013): 916–26.

Garrett W. Meigs, Daniel C. Donato, John L. Campbell, Jonathan G. Martin, and Beverly E. Law, "Forest Fire Impacts on Carbon Uptake, Storage, and Emission: The Role of Burn Severity in the Eastern Cascades, Oregon," *Ecosystems* 12, no. 8 (2009): 1246–67.

Garrett W. Meigs, Harold S. J. Zald, John L. Campbell, William S. Keeton, Robert E. Kennedy, "Do Insect Outbreaks Reduce the Severity of Subsequent Forest Fires?" *Environmental Research Letters* 11, no. 4 (2016): 045008.

W. W. Oswald, D. R. Foster, B. N. Shuman, et al., "Conservation Implications of Limited Native American Impacts in Pre-Contact New England," *Nature Sustainability* 3 (2020): 241–46.

——, "Reply," *Nature Sustainability* 3 (2020): 900–903.

S. J. Prichard et al., "Adapting Western North American Forests to Climate Change and Wildfires: 10 Common Questions," *Ecological Applications* 31, no. 8 (2021): https://doi:10.1002/eap.2433.

Eric Rutkow, "Forests of Commerce," *American Canopy: Trees, Forests, and the Making of a Nation*, 1st ed. (New York: Scribner, 2012): 115–20.

Charlene Sharpe, "Proposed Timber Harvesting Questioned," *Maryland Coast Dispatch*, March 18, 2021, https://mdcoastdispatch.com/2021/03/18/proposed-timber-harvesting-questioned/.

Jeffrey E. Stenzel, Kristina J. Bartowitz, Melannie D. Hartman, James A. Lutz, Crystal A. Kolden, Alistair M. S. Smith, Beverly E. Law, et al., "Fixing a Snag in Carbon Emissions Estimates from Wildfires," *Global Change Biology* 25, no. 11 (2019): 3985–94.

J. R. Thompson and T. A. Spies, "Factors Associated with Crown Damage Following Recurring Mixed-Severity Wildfires and Post-Fire Management in Southwestern Oregon," *Landscape Ecology* 25 (2010): 775–89.

Simon Thorn, Bässler Claus, Roland Brandl, Philip J. Burton, Rebecca Cahall, John L. Campbell, Jorge Castro, et al., "Impacts of Salvage Logging on Biodiversity: A Meta-Analysis." *Journal of Applied Ecology* 55, no. 1 (2018): 279–89.

18 The Largest Trees (pages 181–193)

Detailed instructions for measuring Champion Tree candidates are given in *American Forests Champion Trees Measuring Guidelines Handbook*, by Robert T. Leverett and Dan Bertolette, available at https://americanforests .org/wp-content/uploads/2014/12/AF-Tree-Measuring-Guidelines_LR.pdf.

George Washington's reference to the large sycamore is in his November 4, 1770, diary entry.

The Ridgway measurements are documented in the *Proceedings of the United States National Museum* 5 (June 1882), while a record of Ridgway's account of the large sycamore appears in *The Journal of Heredity* 6 (1915).

For early photographs of forests, see the Forest History Society's photograph collection at https://foresthistory.org/Research/photos.html.

Al C. Carder, *Forest Giants of the World* (Markham, Ontario: FitzHenry and Whiteside, 1995).

Gordon G. Whitney, *From Coastal Wilderness to Fruited Plain: A History of Environmental Change in Temperate North America from 1500 to the Present* (Cambridge, England: Cambridge University Press, 1994).

Index

trees (*continued*)
services of, 139–40; emergent supercanopy, 133; fallen, and forest structural diversity, 3; growth rate and carbon dioxide absorption of, 160–62; hub, 95–96; largest, 184, 186; measurement of, 187–90; oldest on Earth, 27–29, 182; in old-growth versus younger forest, 2–3; as partners to mosses and liverworts, 87–88; production of new species of, 8; relationship between fungi and, 94–96; role of large and old, in forest ecology, 17–18; shrinkage of, 183; size of, 162, 184; effects of size of, 88, 162; suppression of, 172; tallest species of, 182, 184; transpiration and, 150
Triodopsis tridentata, 50
tulip poplars, 184, 185

University of Alaska Fairbanks, 93–94
University of British Columbia, 95

van Helmont, Jan Baptista, 157
Van Pelt, Robert, 189
Viburnum alnifolium, 75, 77
Viola blanda, 78
virgin forests, 1

walks in the forest, benefits of, 142–43

wars, 142
water cycle, forests and, 140, 149–55
white ash, Adirondack Park, 88
white cedars, 80, 108–9
white oaks, 17, 57–58
white pines, 133, 185–87
wildfires: after-effects of, 178, 180; fuel for, 172–73; human causes of, 176, 177; indicators of, 171; in old-growth forests, 175–76
wild forests, 32–33, 87
wild sarsaparilla, 77
wind, 150–51, 174
winter wren, 35, 36
Wizard of Oz Memorial Oak Grove, North Syracuse, New York, 18
wolves, 135
wood-air bathing (*shinrin-yoku*), 142–43
wood frog, 42
woodland ground beetles, 43, 66
wood products, and carbon sequestration, 163
worm-composting project, 125–26
worm-eating warblers, 32
worms: native, 120–22; nonnative/invasive, 120, 123–28
Wyatt, Julie, 77–78, 82

yellow-bellied flycatchers, 35–36

Zald, Harold, 175